Petra Schneider

LightBeings
Master Essences

A Path to Mastering Life
A Systematic Introduction to the Energy
of the Ascended Masters

Translated by Christine M. Grimm

ARCANA
PUBLISHING

LightBeings Master Essences do not make the visit to a doctor, naturopath, or psychotherapist superfluous when there is suspicion of a serious health disorder.

The information in this book has been presented to the best of our knowledge and conscience. Despite this fact, the authors do not assume any liability whatsoever for damages of any type that may occur through the direct or indirect application of the LightBeings Master Essences or utilization of the statements in this book.

"LightBeings" and "Master Essences" are protected trademarks by Dr. Petra Schneider.

1st English edition 1998
© by Arcana Publishing
    Box 325, Twin Lakes, WI 53181
Published in cooperation
with Schneelöwe Verlagsberatung, Federal Republic of Germany
© 1997 reserved by the Windpferd Verlagsgesellschaft mbH, Aitrang
All rights reserved
Translated by Christine M. Grimm
Cover design by Kuhn Grafik, Digitales Design, Zurich
Illustrations: Ute Rossow
Make-up: *panta rhei!* – MediaService Uwe Hiltmann
Production: Schneelöwe, D-87648 Aitrang

ISBN 0-910261-18-0
Library of Congress Catalogue No. 97-78482

Printed in the USA

LightBeings
Master Essences

Contents

Part 3—Description of the 21 Master Energies

Do you see the moon up there?
Only half of it can be seen
And yet it's round and lovely
That's how some things are
That we laugh at confidently
Because our eyes don't see them.

FROM: THE MOON HAS RISEN
MATTHIAS CLAUDIUS, 1778

Introduction

"Call the essences 'LightBeings Master Essences'."

When we heard this while channeling*, our first response was to resist. We had already learned through our work that the essences help in mastering life. Since consciousness in everyday life is the central issue here, we thought they should be labeled with a name that sounds spiritual and exalted, indicating that these are the essences of the "Ascended Masters"—from Light-Beings, intangible and invisible beings.

However, we had misunderstood the name: "You are the Light-Beings. Every human is a light-filled being. And the essences support you in becoming the master of your own life."

The work with the Master Essences deals with our life and our self. It involves seeing what hinders us in making full use of our potential and living our true being. The essences support us in perceiving why we block ourselves again and again, putting obstacles in our own path, building snares and traps into our life, and why we can't manage to lead a lastingly successful, relaxed, happy, and conscious life.

The suggestion that we work with the "Ascended Masters" came as a result of our channeling, and we had no idea what was waiting for us. We had already worked with subtle energies for a number of years, and had gained access to higher levels of consciousness.

However, we hadn't yet had any direct contact with the "Ascended Masters." With a curious, joyful, and open attitude we began—and were guided through an intensive process that increasingly led us to ourselves.

---

* A "channel" is a person who is capable of receiving mediumistic messages by extending his consciousness to another level of consciousness. The medium goes beyond the boundaries of ego consciousness and the mind in order to receive and impart information, images, or energy from and into other levels of consciousness.
The channeled information in this book came from the Ascended Masters.

We experienced highs and lows and times of doubt and wonder. There was pain and joy. We had financial problems because the production of the "LightBeings Master Essences" swallowed up much more money that we had imagined—and we received unexpected help. Over and over again we had doubts about what we were doing and thought about whether it just might be nonsense. Then the enthusiastic responses came from people who had tried out the essences.

Much happened within us as well: Every aspect of our lives was turned upside down and purified. We came up against fears, negative expectations, and unloved aspects of ourselves that we had suppressed. We perceived where our true being was hidden behind masks.

Sometimes it was difficult for us to look at and integrate our unloved aspects. Yet, we always felt the loving, unconditional support of the "masters." The essences strengthened the inner certainty that we would succeed. Even when things became very difficult, we had the courage to go on and felt our inner strength.

So we are at a point today where we live a more fulfilled life. Full of gratitude, we look at our development and the help and support that we have received. In retrospect we see that we have achieved more quality of life and consciousness in a very quick and unusually easy way. We have become more authentic, self-confident, cheerful, and content, looking at our life in a more conscious way. We have learned, and are still learning, to stand with both feet in life and on the ground, to love the world and be more conscious of ourselves in the greater correlations and in our divine being. We live "spirituality in everyday life."

And the two of us agree: We both would take the same path again.

A Brief Survey
of this Book's Structure

This book consists of three parts:
- The Fundamentals of Working with Subtle Energies
- The Work with LightBeings Master Essences
- Description of the 21 Master Energies

The Fundamentals of Working with Subtle Energies contains information on the Master Essences, the Ascended Masters, and the "esoteric view of the world." There are various models of the subtle energy system, and each model has its justification. We have therefore provided a brief description of the model with which we work.

For people who have had little previous contact with the subtle energy system, the fundamentals section can serve as an introduction. If necessary, they will find more extensive information in other books regarding the themes touched on here.

The Work with LightBeings Master Essences describes the effects and applications of the essences, as well as providing some techniques for the work of increasing consciousness.

The Description of the 21 Master Energies serves as a reference work in which you can find a summary of the effects of the essences, as well as the symptoms of the balanced and blocked states. This chapter also contains an extensive description of all the Master Essences, their association with the chakras, colors, Tarot cards, and gemstones, as well as channeled meditation instructions and a channeled message for each of them.

In the *Appendix*, you will find answers to the most frequently asked questions and a brief description of the master energies.

We would like to make one more comment on the description of the "subtle view of the world," which includes the themes of the subtle energy system, the effect of the LightBeings Master Essences, the explanation of waking consciousness, the unconscious mind, the Higher Self and higher levels of consciousness, disease, and past lives. The explanations of these themes are models of reality. Such models make complex correlations, the direct description of which is impossible for us, easier to grasp and comprehensible with familiar *images*. Models have limitations. They can only give a rough sketch of a reality. A car is more than a coach without horses that makes a loud sound while driving and emits a cloud of smoke behind it. However, for a person who is only familiar with coaches and horses, this description is a help in imagining what a car is like.

The description of the subtle view of the world is also a picture that illustrates reality.

Part 1

The Background—
Fundamentals of Working
with Subtle Energies

Chapter 1

What are LightBeings Master Essences?

Support on the Path to Being Healed

The LightBeings Master Essences are a tool for self-knowledge, for becoming more aware, for developing consciousness, and for self-realization. The goal of work with the Master Essences is to perceive your own true core and live your very own being in everyday life. They are a way to achieve your own mastery. Consciousness develops more and more on this path, and your own potential can be put to full use. The essences support us in living a successful and fulfilled life.

As is also the case for other paths of developing consciousness, through the work with the Master Essences we increasingly experience who we are, what masks we wear, behind which limitations, patterns of behavior, games, or avoidance strategies we hide ourselves. We recognize what hinders us from living what we really want to live. The Master Essences help us to focus our eyes directly on our potential. They help us see what we want to live and what stops us from doing this: our blocks. The essences reactivate the potential that is already within us, but which we haven't developed up to now. At the same time, they are comparable with the Zen stick of the Zen master that purposefully strikes the meditating person at the right moment and with the proper intensity. The Zen stick serves to make the meditating person attentive again in those moments when he is no longer conscious. It isn't a punishment, but rather a loving aid. The stick is never too hard, but it can be painful.

The Zen master only uses the stick when the student has given him permission to do so beforehand. Our inner willingness decides the effect of the essences in the same way.

The Master Essences bring light into the dark, into our un-loved shadow aspects. Sometimes we may become frightened about what we recognize there. Yet, by consciously seeing and accepting it, we are *healed*. What we had previously shut out, what we hadn't wanted to see, and what stopped us from devel-oping ourselves—all of this now can allow us to become *whole*.

But not just the Master Essence alone determines how strong the effect is. The reactions are also shaped by the inner resist-ance and the user's conscious and unconscious willingness to reflect about himself and grow as a result. When we want to know a great deal and grow quickly, the reactions can turn out to be more vehement than when we take our time. Just like we can either choose to travel on the hiking path or climb the steep slope to the peak of a mountain. However, sometimes we are still surprised by the intensity of the events—or we expect a ve-hement reaction and it doesn't happen. Then we have uncon-sciously selected another path than the one we consciously be-lieved we chose.

The Master Essences support us on our path. They guide our vision and are teachers that make us attentive. They open our eyes, give us energy, dissolve blocks, and strengthen our confi-dence so that we can walk the path more easily. Yet, we must walk it ourselves.

The 21 Master Essences represent 21 fundamental themes in life or soul qualities that we would like to learn.

What's in the Essences?

The 21 LightBeings Master Essences contain the pure spiritual subtle vibration of 21 Ascended Masters. The effect of the es-sences isn't based on earthly forms of being such as plants or gemstones. In order for the spiritual information to become ef-fective in the material form, the vibration is attached to matter, which means to oil or water in this case.

The image of the "supportive entities" and the "Ascended Masters" is a model of reality. You don't have to believe in the "Ascended Masters" for the essences to have an effect—just as little as you have to believe in gemstones or colors in order to achieve a reaction with them. The explanations serve to help the rational mind. However, they are not necessary for the sake of effectiveness and success. The essences have an effect through the subtle energy vibrations contained within them. When we speak of the "energy of the masters" in the following, you can simply replace this with the "Master Essences" if the latter corresponds more closely with your view of the world. When working with the essences, you can also use the numbers in place of the master names.

Who Are the Ascended Masters?

The Ascended Masters are energy forms or non-physical entities from higher levels of consciousness (see Chapter 4 "The Lifework") that support human beings in the development of their consciousness. They are familiar with life on earth, with human problems and entanglements, and the path to unity.

Many of these entities have lived on earth and taken this path of development themselves. Lao Tse and Kwan Yin are familiar names, and there has been literature written about them. But the Christ energy can also be easily understood through the Biblical texts. On the basis of stories, we know that these people have taken the "path of enlightenment" and have developed themselves. They have gone through the difficulties of human existence, through the duality, in order to once again attain unity. Now that they have taken this path themselves, they support human beings on their own path.

The esoteric world long been familiar with the entities of the Ascended Masters. Some people presume that they are behind the movements of the Templars, the Freemasons, and the Theosophical Society. Aura-Soma and members of the "Great White Brotherhood" organization work with the energies of the Ascended Masters.

The names of some of the masters have been recorded in the books by Helena Blavatsky and Alice Bailey, who were both born at the end of the previous (19th) century.

The group of the Ascended Masters includes more than 21 entities. Not all of them have been incarnated on the earth, yet—

because of their love of humanity—all of them have taken on the task of supporting human beings on their path of consciousness. For this purpose, they have joined their experiences and their knowledge into a mutual consciousness, to which each master has access. All masters are thereby connected with the life of human beings. They are familiar with human weaknesses and strengths, with the entanglements, hopes, difficulties, obstacles, possibilities, and apparent limitations—simply everything that is related to human life. They know exactly how they can support individual people in their growth. And this is what they have seen as their task ever since the human being has taken the path of increasing consciousness.

The meaning of the term "Ascended Masters" can best be explained with the metaphor of the "Ascension of Christ": the human being Jesus increasingly dissolved his ego-definition and ultimately united himself with the Christ consciousness. On his path on earth he also transformed his physical body and expanded his consciousness so extensively that his body became "light." This body was then no longer subject to the limitations of matter. With the light-body he had the possibility of appearing and disappearing again at any time (see the biblical stories of Jesus's appearances after his death on the cross). People could see and even touch him (the Apostle Thomas placed his fingers in the wounds on Jesus's body). This is how all Ascended Masters have the possibility of creating an earthly body for themselves.

There are also reports that other masters have appeared on the earth. In the 18th century, Saint Germain encountered a great variety of personalities during the time period spanning almost 100 years, teaching and supporting human beings. He was always described as a man who was about 45-years-old.

The question arises why the masters have brought their energy into the essences at this point in time and why specifically these 21 master energies are contained within them, although there are more than 21 Ascended Masters.

Humanity is living in a time of profound change. A transition is underway from the Age of Pisces, which has the water element and emotions associated with it, to the Age of Aquarius, which has its emphasis on the air element and therefore the mental level. At this time, many entities and energy forms such the angels and archangels, for example, are supporting the development of humanity.

The 21 masters present themselves as those who are involved with the development of life themes. We could compare these masters with the archetypes or also with the developmental path of a human being depicted in the Major Arcana of the Tarot. If we consider the Master Essences in the order of the numbers, the themes are built upon each other. No. 21—*Mary* concludes a cycle of development and leads on to the next level, which once again starts with No. 1—*Maha Chohan*. This can also be compared with a spiral that turns upwards or a winding staircase. One life theme is lived through and experienced over and over again on the different levels of the spiral. As a result, the 21 Master Essences also represent an evolution of consciousness through 21 steps. With each passage of a cycle, we come closer to the core of our own being.

Chapter 2

The Origin of the LightBeings Master Essences

A Brief Insight into a Long Story

When I (Petra) received the instructions to work with the Ascended Masters while channeling, I had been aware of them, although I had never had direct contact with them.

Years before, just as I was beginning my spiritual path, a channeled book from Saint Germain had fallen into my hands in a small esoteric book store. It had magically attracted me, and the name sounded very familiar to my ears, although I had never heard of it before and couldn't imagine what it meant. As I held it in my hand, I felt a tingling within me. The pleasant tension that I felt reminded me of the feeling before a rendezvous. "Strange," I thought to myself and opened it. However, the texts were difficult to read and I could hardly understand the contents. So I put the book back on the shelf.

A short time later I found out who Saint Germain is and what the "Ascended Masters" are at a lecture held by the "White Brotherhood" (a spiritual organization). I also felt myself drawn to him here, along with a heartfelt sense of familiarity with the masters. Yet, I wasn't that far at that moment.

In the following period of time, I became acquainted with Gerhard and we both began to work with subtle energies. I discovered my ability to channel.

The next time I encountered the master energies was at a seminar. There were little plastic bottles with colored liquids on the table, which magically attracted me. I read the names on the labels—they were the names of the Ascended Masters. Once again, they evoked within me a feeling of intimacy and familiarity, an inner tingling, and a pleasant shiver. These were the Quintessences by Aura-Soma. And suddenly I knew: "At some point

I will work with these masters." And this thought filled me with a vast sense of happiness.

At first, the masters slipped my mind again and two years past before things got moving. Once again, this was triggered by the Aura-Soma Quintessences. Gerhard and I began to work with them.

A short time later, while channeling, we then received the instructions to bind the energy of the masters to matter.

My rational mind rebelled at first: "But I can't do that. How should I do something like that? Maybe other people can do it, but I can't." Yet, at the same time this thought fascinated both of us and we became involved with this process. The result was a time of intensive growth and transformation.

The entire procedure of the charging process, the preparations, the rituals and techniques, were transmitted to us. We began making our own essences and working with them.

Before we could charge the energy of a master, we had to prepare ourselves. This meant purifying ourselves of inner blocks and attuning ourselves. We used our charged oils and tinctures every day, meditated with the energies of the respective master, channeled and experienced his energy and what it evoked within us. It took between 12 days and 2 months, depending on how many blocks we ourselves had on this theme, before we could create the space for the master so that he could bind his energy to the oil and water.

This time with the master energies was among the most intensive transformational processes in our lives. I noticed, for example, that I had a distinct tendency of "disappearing from the earth" and being unrealistic. Since it wasn't enough to just charge the essences, I had to take care of things that got *my feet firmly on the ground*. There were suddenly questions: Where do we get the bottles? Which oils can we use? How can we mix them? How do we design the label? Where do we get the alcohol for the tinctures?

I saw that the *subtle* work is just one part of reality, and after initial resistance, I also began to love the *earthly* work. I found a way to combine both with each other. And I started to enjoy my life in this body.

In retrospect, it has been astonishing for me to experience the help and guidance we have received in this process over and over again. We had no idea of the production steps and only afterwards did we learn about what could have gone wrong. But everything worked out. Things happened that we call wonders. We knew that the essences wanted to be "born" in mid-November of 1995. Although it didn't look like this could succeed, it happened. At the end of November the essences were in two esoteric stores.

We were naturally overcome with doubts time and again: "Are we just imagining all of this? Isn't it just wishful thinking that the essences have an effect?" After some of the essences had been made, we gave them to various people for testing. The feedback was so tremendous that we had the courage to continue our work and produce the essences.

Don't believe that the doubts disappeared after the initial feedback. They returned time and again. At first, I just couldn't and wouldn't believe that the essences had such a strong effect. Yet, whenever I was at the point of giving up, friends encouraged us or an enthusiastic reaction reached us. And this is how it still is today. Although we don't advertise our essences at the moment, there are inquiries and enthusiastic telephone calls.

In the meantime, we have recognized that this process concerns the development of our own consciousness above everything else. In a relatively short amount of time, we both have gone through many layers of our being. Much healing, transformation, and growth on all levels has occurred through the master energy.

And we continue in this process since our goal is to completely develop and live out our existence.

How We Make the LightBeings Master Essences

The LightBeings Master Essences contain the energy vibrations of the Ascended Masters. In order to bind these vibrations to a material substance, thorough preparation and attunement is required. After the preparation period, the respective master energy is bound to water and oil.

The substances produced in this step serve as original essences.

All steps of the preparation and production were transmitted to us in detail by the masters during channeling.

In the selection of the base substances, we pay attention to a high level of quality. The tincture contains a mixture of purified water and pure alcohol (ethyl alcohol). For the oils we use pure cold-pressed oils of edible-oil quality.

The essential oils are selected by a well-known aromatherapist so that they support the effects of the energy vibration. They are supplied by a company that emphasizes a high level of quality and purity.

Before the production process, all the materials are cleansed energetically. This includes the equipment with which we work and the bottles, the oils, the alcohol, and the water. They are prepared in such a way that nothing remains of their own vibration or outside vibrations.

After filling, all of the bottles and energy balls are sealed so that they don't take on any outside vibrations. The essences and balls can therefore be used by several people at the same or passed on to others.

The entire production process, including the filling, is done by hand. The containers in all production steps are made of glass. In energetic terms, these are the best preconditions for a high level of quality.

Chapter 3

Fundamentals and Correlations Between the Material World and the Subtle World

The Subtle Body of the Human Being

A subtle energy system exists along with the dense matter of the physical body. Energy makes it possible for a system to do its work, and the term "energy" is usually used in this way. However, at the same time every energy vibration also contains information, just like a newspaper simultaneously has a fuel value and conveys information. Through the transmission of information, functional processes like the activity of the heart, the digestion, and hormone production in the body are controlled, just to name a few examples.

In order for the body to work in a healthy way, it needs control information and work energy. With the work energy, it can react to the control impulses. When we speak of energy in the following, this always refers to both information energy and work energy.

The subtle human energy system surrounds and traverses the physical body and is invisible for most people. It's composed of three parts:
• The energy paths
• The energy bodies
• The chakras

These parts of the energy system penetrate and mutually influence each other, as well as the physical body. The so-called subtle energy flows through them.

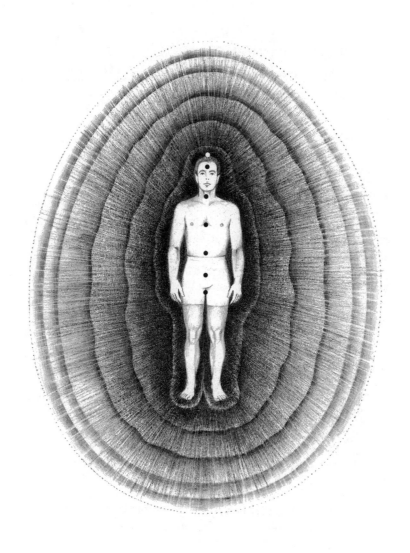

Aura layers and chakras

The Energy Paths

Just as the body is traversed by blood streams, all of which deliver material parts of oxygen and nutrients, it's also supplied with subtle energy through the energy paths. These energy paths are also called meridians. Subtle energy is life energy, which is called *prana* in Indian, *qi* or *chi* in Chinese, and *ki* in Japanese.

Life energy is what keeps us and every other living being alive through work energy and information energy. When we no longer take in life energy and also have no more reserves of it within our body, our body becomes lifeless—which means dead.

We take in the life energy by breathing, through our food, and by way of the chakras.

The energy paths (meridians) connect the organ systems with each other and supply the entire body with the necessary life energy. When an unhindered flow of energy is possible and we take in enough energy, we are physically healthy and also in good shape psychologically. However, if there are disorders or blocks in the energy flow, certain parts of the body are undersupplied as a result.

Using the image of a river system, we can easily understand the correlations. If the rivers are open and have enough water in them, the vegetation around them turns green and blossoms. The land is adequately supplied. However, if the course of a river is blocked by something like a landslide, the areas beyond it no longer receive adequate water. At first, this is hardly visible, but then the plants begin to wilt and finally die after a certain period of time.

Our body also reacts in this way when the energy paths are blocked. After a period of time, the inadequately supplied body parts or organs no longer function. They lack in work energy and information. At first, slight complaints occur, which are often overlooked. Later, diseases develop.

The Energy Bodies

Our body is enveloped and traversed by a number of subtle energy fields, which are called *aura bodies*. The aura bodies differ in size and vibrational frequency.

The first energy field corresponds to the body's contours in its form, but all further aura layers tend to resemble the shape of an egg. They become increasingly large in their extension and have finer vibrations. The first aura layer has very low vibrations, and the last layer has the highest frequency. If we compare them to colors, the first energy body corresponds to the color red and the seventh corresponds to ultraviolet.

Above all, the first six aura layers are related to existence here on earth. The seventh body connects us with higher levels of consciousness. Beyond these are still further aura layers. However, a description of them would go beyond the scope of this book.

The Ethereal Body

The first aura layer is called the ethereal body and has the shape of our body, but is about 5 to 15 centimeters larger. Its size is dependent on the human being's condition and his supply of life energy. The ethereal body has the most dense vibrations and represents a state between energy and matter. It's therefore easy to perceive the ethereal body, and many people can see it. Its appearance is like a grayish or whitish flickering around the body.

The ethereal body has the closest contact with the physical body and connects it with the subtle levels. It receives life energy (ki or chi) through the solar plexus chakra (3rd chakra), as well as earth energy from the base chakra (1st chakra), passing it on to the physical body through the chakras and energy paths.

The Emotional Body

The second aura body has the vibrational frequency with the second highest density. It passes through the ethereal body and the physical body. Since it sustains and controls all the feelings, we call it the emotional body. Basic qualities like anger, sadness, fear, joy, and feelings of desire exist within the emotional body.

It extends from 30 to 50 centimeters beyond the body.

We always feel the boundaries of our emotional body in daily life when someone "gets too close" to us and enters into our emotional body with his own. We usually *feel* ourselves unpleasantly touched and automatically move away a bit in these situations. It's different with people we like or with whom we have already lived for a long time like the intimate partner, children, or parents. When they come close to us, we usually have a pleasant feeling.

The emotional body most strongly influences the average person in his behavior and view of the world. In addition to pleasant emotional experiences, it stores all the disagreeable experiences in life like fears, aggressions, being rejected, a lack of self-confidence, and so forth. According to how we feel, we radiate a certain energy frequency that other people perceive unconsciously. They sense whether we are happy or sad, and react accordingly. This is why we usually attract other cheerful people when we are happy and vice verse.

The feelings that we suppress and no longer perceive ourselves are also radiated to the outside world. As a result, we then attract people who have precisely the same behavior or behavior similar to what we don't want to see within ourselves. We often become terribly irritated about these other people instead of recognizing ourselves in them and using them as a mirror.

Examples of disorders in the emotional body are suppressed, unlived feelings. The effect of disorders and blocks is that we don't feel well. If the flow of energy is balanced, we feel good, harmonized, and full of the joy of life.

The Mental Body

The third aura body is called the mental body. All thoughts, ideas, conscious and unconscious thinking processes, and rational and intuitive perceptions take place within it. Memories are stored here. It contains beliefs, moral ideals, valuations, and controls the behavior patterns according to which we live. The mental body extends up to one meter beyond the physical body. It carries on an intensive exchange with the brain.

The mental body processes sensory impressions.

It has one further significant task: It translates the impulses of the Higher Self, which come through the spiritual body.

Since the energy field of the mental body penetrates that of the emotional body, the ethereal body, and the physical body, there is a strong interaction between them. When we have a negative thought, a change in our feelings and physical posture takes place immediately.

If you would like to try this out, imagine in full detail an encounter with an unpleasant person upon whom you are dependent. Observe your posture, your breathing, and your emotions at the same time.

Now think of an experience in which you were very successful and powerful. How are you sitting or standing now? How are you breathing? How do you feel?

These areas have a direct influence on each other: Through thoughts like: "I can't accomplish this, it's too much work," stress leads to oppressive feelings and physical reactions like hormonal secretions. These hormones have the purpose of making us take flight and therefore restrict our ability to think. As a result, we then wind up under even more pressure. People who live with such thoughts over a longer period of time imprint them as patterns in the aura layer. The energy flow becomes blocked, and this can ultimately lead to diseases like ulcers, migraine headaches, and heart attacks.

But this process works in the reverse direction as well. People who think: "I can get this done," despite the mountain of work in front of them feel well, have more energy available, and don't become ill despite the work.

The Spiritual Aura Body

The fourth aura body is called the astral body and extends from one to 1.5 meters beyond the physical body. It forms a bridge between the aura bodies beneath it, above all with those connected to our current life on earth, and the higher aura bodies, which are primarily related to our cosmic or divine existence.

Aura bodies four to seven are frequently summarized under the term of "spiritual aura bodies."

The Chakras

In addition to the meridians and the aura bodies, the chakras are a part of the energy system. They are the gateways between the meridians and the aura, transmitting both energy and information.

For this purpose, they take energy from the physical body, the aura bodies, and from the surrounding environment, and transform and pass it on to the energy paths and the aura bodies.

Chakra is a Sanskrit word and means "energy wheel." People who can see auras have described them as colored wheels that turn at various speeds. Altogether, there are many thousands of such energy-reception centers within the body. However, most of them are very small.

The most important chakras are the seven main chakras, which are arranged along the center line of the body. In addition, there are further main chakras above the head and about forty larger secondary chakras within the body.

The seven main chakras are linked with the seven major hormonal glands of the body (Köhler). Each chakra supplies various organs and parts of the body with energy, correlating with various life themes.

In the following is a survey of their association with the body and the life themes.

First Chakra—Root Chakra

Theme: Fundamental survival functions and needs, connection to the earth energy, preservation of the species, fighting ability, and assertive power.
Location: Pelvic floor, radiates downwards.
Related organs: Spinal column, bones, nails, teeth, legs, and adrenal glands.

Second Chakra—Sacral Chakra

Theme: Sexuality and sensuality, joy in life, likes and aversions, relationships, and appetite and digestion.
Location: In front about three fingers below the navel and at the corresponding level in the back.

Related organs: Reproductive organs, kidneys, digestion, skin, and everything fluid within the body.

Third Chakra—Solar Plexus Chakra

Theme: Personal will, power, dominance, fear, and processing of feelings and experiences.

Location: Midway between the end of the sternum and the navel at the corresponding level in the back.

Related organs: Liver, stomach, gallbladder, pancreas, autonomic nervous system, joints, musculature in a state of tension, energy metabolism, and detoxification through elimination.

Fourth Chakra—Heart Chakra

Theme: Connective point between spirit and matter, heaven and earth, ability to love unconditionally, harmony, empathy, ability to concentrate, and healing.

Location: In the front close to the lower tip at the breast bone and at the corresponding level in the back.

Related organs: Heart, lungs, circulation, thymus gland, musculature in a state of relaxation, and detoxification through deposits in the fatty depot.

Fifth Chakra—Throat Chakra

Theme: Communication, self-expression, creativity, inspiration, and individuality.

Location: At the front in the larynx area and at the corresponding level in the back,

Related organs: Throat, neck, thyroid gland, voice, larynx, bronchial tubes, lungs, equilibrium between physical and mental growth.

Sixth Chakra—Forehead Chakra or Third Eye

Theme: Looking inwards, inner knowledge, seeing higher truths, intuition, perception of one's own path in the cosmic context, and perception of the self.

Location: At the front between the eyebrows and above the bridge of the nose and at the corresponding level in the back.

Related organs: Nose, ears, eyes, face, cerebellum, pituitary gland.

Seventh Chakra—Crown Chakra

Theme: Uniting with transpersonal or higher consciousness, spirituality, self-realization, cosmic consciousness, and transformation.
Location: Top of the head, only radiates upwards.
Related organs: Cerebrum, pineal gland.

The Hara

The hara isn't a chakra. The term comes from the Japanese language—this center isn't specified in the Indian chakra system. Its location is about three fingers below the navel and is also called the "life and death center." This is the point that is opened in the Japanese ritual suicide—hara-kiri. Life leaks out very quickly here.

The hara is the center of vital power and life energy. Among other things, its task is to stabilize the energy system and the immune system.

Causes of Disorders and Blocks in the Energy System

In the section on the energy paths, the example of a disrupted river system was used to illustrate the effects of blocks. This also applies to the chakras and aura bodies. Each disorder restricts the flow of energy and changes the vibrational frequency.

Disorders in the energy system occur through restrictions that we take on from the surrounding world, because of unpleasant suppressed experiences, and as a result of deviations from the life plan.

Disorders Resulting from the Environment

We are born into a specific environment and accept its values, beliefs, and concepts. Beliefs are generalizations about the causes, meaning, and boundaries of the world. They have the effect of a filter through which we perceive the world since they fade or color certain things. They influence our behavior, our abilities, and our self-image.

There are supportive and inhibitive beliefs. Supportive beliefs permit us to try out and use our abilities: "nothing ventured, nothing gained," "practice makes perfect," and "you can do it." Examples of inhibitive beliefs are: "life is hard," "there's no such thing as a free lunch, "money rules the world," or many proverbs and common sayings that we adopt: "don't count your chickens before they hatch," "the biter will be the bitten," "the early-bird gets the worm," "you can't teach an old dog new tricks," and so forth.

Among these beliefs are also the concepts we have about ourselves: "that always happens to me" or "I can't do that, I'll never learn."

Since our parents and our surrounding world generally live with restrictive beliefs, we adopt them in time and shape our life in accordance with them.

Have you ever thought about how children learn to walk? How they never tire of it, imperturbably get up over and over again when they have fallen down, and keep on trying until they can do it? Falling down isn't a failure for them! They try until they succeed. They have adults as their role models and not a bit of doubt about their own ability to learn.

However, in the course of the years our attitude about unsuccessful attempts usually changes. We adopt the opinion held by other people that it's bad to make mistakes, that we should give up if the expected success doesn't happen the first time around— or at least after a few attempts. How quickly do you give up today when you start something new? Would you still learn to walk today with this attitude?

And what would be different in your life if you would act like a small child according to the motto: "What other people achieve, I can do as well. Even if I fall down again and again in the meantime—I'm happy about every little bit of progress"?

Here is another example of blocks in the energy system through influences in the surrounding world: A child lives its vital energy, is boisterous and wild, and constantly hears sentences like: "Watch out, you're going to fall down," "Don't be so wild," "You're going to hurt yourself," or is even punished for its wildness (we could also call it the "free flowing of its vital energy"). It ultimately begins to subdue its energy. When very little energy flows and the child is quiet, it's praised for being a "well-behaved child." So it learns to hold back its energy, stores this pattern, and thereby unconsciously blocks the flow of energy.

Statements by other "authorities" can also create blocks. A friend told me how she had pain in her knee at the age of sixteen. An examination revealed that there was a slight deviation in the knee, and the doctor told her that as long as she engaged in sports she would have no symptoms. However, if she stopped, the pain would return and the knee could even become stiff. Since she still went to school at that time and enjoyed sports, the pain soon disappeared. However, when she stopped her sport activities after the birth of her first child, the pain began again. She wasn't surprised since the doctor had predicted this. It was only after we had talked about such blocks that it occurred to her that she possibly wouldn't have pain without sports, that this physical reaction was possibly created by her pattern of belief that "no sports means pain." She dissolved this pattern, and the pain disappeared without her doing any sports—and never returned.

Particularly statements by doctors as authorities create energy patterns within us that have an unconscious effect. How often do I hear people say: "My doctor said that this will never improve, that I have to live with it," "In two years this must be operated on," "If my blood pressure doesn't do down, I'll have a heart attack," "This disease is incurable," "This disease is hereditary"—and how much of this actually occurs just because we believe it will? These sentences effect our subconscious mind and can become reality through their energetic effects.

These examples show how restrictive beliefs can cause disorders and blocks in the flow of our energy. This in turn influences our thoughts, feelings, and ultimately our health. Emotional shocks, undigested and suppressed experiences have the same effect.

A deviation from the plan in life, from what we have resolved to do in this life, also leads to disorders.

Here is an example of this: a person has planned to learned leadership behavior in this life. However, he constantly holds back and doesn't express his needs, choosing a profession in which he only carries out orders. As a result, he avoids the learning task and creates disorders in the flow of energy. This initially has an effect on the mental body: he frequently thinks about this theme. Then he begins to suffer because of his powerlessness, and physical complaints ultimately occur. He develops stomachaches, then problems with his pancreas, and so forth. The disorder is slight at first and becomes increasingly distinct—yet the correlation with the cause is probably no longer recognizable for this person.

Restrictive concepts change the flow of energy in the body. They prevent us from developing and living our potential.

For example: When a woman has planned to develop her femininity, this becomes difficult if she has the self-image of being a "sweet little girl." It was right for her to live with this image until the time of puberty, and the flow of energy was harmonious. However, if she misses the step of developing into a woman and changing her self-image, disorders will occur. The result may be menstrual complaints or hormonal disorders, for example.

What was fitting in the past and harmonized with the life plan can become inappropriate at a later date.

The LightBeings Master Essences make us aware of such restrictive beliefs, help dissolve blocks in the energy system, and support us in perceiving our own plan in life and living in harmony with it.

What is the Purpose of Disease?

Disease knows just one goal:
to let us be healed.
DETHLEFSEN AND DAHLKE

Disorders in the energy system restrict the natural flow of energy and can therefore cause disease.

Disease means abandoning a previously balanced order. Disease indicates that the person is no longer in harmony with his consciousness, that it's time to go beyond restrictive beliefs. The disorder manifests itself in the body as a symptom of disease. The symptom is the body's language that draws the person's attention and shows him the existing blocks and the change required. The body's symptom isn't a coincidence. There is a direct correlation with the disorder.

Our language shows that this influencing of mind and body has been obvious since ancient times: Someone "is fed up" or "has a bellyful" and "is hopping mad," his "heart is heavy" (sadness), "something turns his stomach" (fright), something is biting him (annoyance influences the liver), "he sees red" or "he foams and fumes" (anger, annoyance), "things get under his skin" (fear, unresolved problems), and "he's itching for a fight."

When we recognize the symptom as a signpost, we can stop seeing disease as the energy that we must fight and destroy. We discover the symptom to be a friend, a teacher who supports us in our own development and path of becoming conscious. Disease shows us the way to "be healed," to increasingly develop our consciousness. If we only cure the symptom but don't heal the cause, it's as if the oil warning lamp lights up in a car and we "repair" this disorder by unscrewing the little lightbulb (from Dethlefsen and Dahlke). This symptom or some other symptom will once again appear after some time.

The cause of disease then lies in the spiritual and mental, subtle area of the human being and not within the physical body. Before a learning step reveals itself as a disorder or symptom in the body, it initially appears in the mental and emotional bodies as a *thought, wish, fantasy, or dream.* If we suppress this impulse, a small, harmless symptom appears: a sense of unwellness, a bad feeling that becomes a functional disorder by way of slight physical disorders. The next step is the acute, physical disorder (for example, inflammation, injury, or minor accidents). When the person doesn't understand the acute demand for change, he will be constantly reminded of it by a *chronic illness.* Chronic processes can produce irreversible physical changes, which are called *incurable diseases* (for example, changes in the organs). Sooner or later, these lead to *death.* What the individual hasn't comprehended before death or during the process of dying, becomes a learning task that is taken into the following incarnation as *karma* (for example, deformities and congenital disease).

The physical disease is therefore the clearest indication of a disorder that constantly becomes more intense if it doesn't receive attention and the cause isn't healed.

In summary, we could say that the meaning of disease is always a spiritual development, a process of becoming whole or healed. Disease is an opportunity to take the pending learning step and resolve karma. The spiritual development then also includes physical healing and vice versa.

On the other hand, we don't have to permit a disease to develop.

As already explained in the previous section, the subtle levels of thoughts and feelings are directly connected with the body. Damage to the organs occurs when the spontaneous thoughts and feelings are suppressed time and again. Instead of flowing freely, the energy is blocked.

In order to once again resolve the symptoms and bottled-up feelings, we often must go through the steps described by Illustration 2 in reverse order and thereby again encounter the formerly bottled-up feelings.

It may be that we suddenly feel sad, angry, or tired without a reason or are reminded of old situations and live through them once again in thoughts, feelings, or dreams. Dreaming is perhaps the body's most common way of working through undigested events and dissolving blocks. This is effective even if we no longer remember our dreams. Intensive dreaming is also a frequent reaction to the use of the Master Essences.

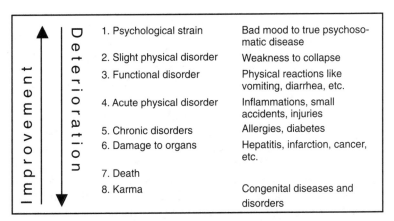

Development of symptoms (according to Köhler, revised)

The illustration summarizes the development of diseases. When the learning step isn't taken, the steps depicted above can be passed through in the order from top to bottom. The healing process goes through these steps in the reverse order. The acute physical disorder becomes a functional disorder. Afterwards, slight physical disorders occur and then the original emotions appear again.

Through the work with the Master Essences, it's easier for the pending learning steps to become conscious. If the learning task is accomplished, the original purpose of the disease becomes invalid and the self-healing process begins. The earlier the learning step is recognized, the less pressure of suffering is necessary.

Past Lives

The image of a person's path through successive lives is a meaningful way of looking at the learning path of consciousness. The question is open as to whether past lives are reality, whether they are inner images that clarify the correlations and support us in perceiving and working on ourselves, or whether they are among a collection of experiences to which we are attached and on which we can fall back on.

The fact is: there is an image world of past lives within us. And these pictures help us to understand events and learning steps. They help us to better deal with destiny and disease since not every *cause* of a disease or blow of fate has necessarily originated within *this* lifetime. However, when the consequences appear during this lifetime (as blows of fate or disease), then the time has come to work through and heal this theme.

The following image may illustrate how the assumption of reincarnation has an effect on understanding the learning path of consciousness: Imagine that a man gets up one morning and has forgotten everything that has taken place in his life up to that point. Then he is very astonished about his headache (from excessive alcohol consumption the evening before), he doesn't understand his lack of money (caused by his extravagant lifestyle), and he is surprised at tenderness from an apparently strange person (who he married some months before). On the other hand, if he knows that he has a past, he also knows why he's in this present state and finds himself in this situation, and he's also familiar with his plans for the future.

The model of reincarnation therefore helps us to understand the correlations and background of the momentary situation and the life. However, it shouldn't be abused in order to shuffle off our responsibility by shifting the causes for difficulties and diseases to past lives.

When we work with the model of reincarnation, we can better understand the correlations and take the pending learning steps. It helps us shape our path of becoming conscious in such a way that we increasingly develop away from the old entanglements of the past and don't create any new ones through unconscious actions. Dethlefsen calls this resolving of karma "eating the fruits of karma."

Our experiences are only complete when we have become familiar with both sides. Whoever was a victim, must then become a perpetrator. Whoever was rich, must become familiar with poverty in order to move beyond both of these extremes, conclude this theme, and define himself as neither a victim nor perpetrator and neither rich nor poor. We have eaten the fruits, and nothing remains. There is emptiness. We overcome the polarity by living through both sides so that we become complete and free. Then we can once again return to the unity.

The Lifework

Waking Consciousness,
Unconscious Mind, and Higher Self

If impulses from the Higher Self reach the waking consciousness, and if the waking consciousness translates the impulses into action, the human being lives in harmony with his lifework and develops his potential.

What are the waking consciousness, the unconscious mind, the Higher Self, and the higher levels of consciousness?

The *waking consciousness* contains everything that we consciously perceive. This includes thought, memory, analysis, logic, and the ability to consciously grasp correlations. It can create goals for the future and understand the past, and also functions as the implementing part of our life.

For example, when we organize a party we use our waking consciousness by making a plan, remembering what we liked about past parties and what was less successful; then we plan and act by inviting people, going shopping, and so forth.

The waking consciousness sees itself as clearly distinct and separate from the whole. And a human being usually identifies with the waking consciousness. The ego—which is also called self-awareness, the conscious self, or personalty—is created on the basis of this differentiation.

The *unconscious mind* is found between the waking consciousness on the one hand and the Higher Self and cosmic consciousness on the other hand. The aspects of the unconscious mind are:

- *Beliefs, patterns of behavior, and experiences* that have sunk down from the waking consciousness and which we no longer remember.

- *Potentials* that we have brought along into this life without being conscious of them such as *abilities* with which we are not yet familiar.
- *Information* that reaches us from the Higher Self and the higher levels of consciousness like *premonitions, visions, and intuitions.*

Some parts of the unconscious mind are called the "inner child, inner healer, inner guide, or inner wisdom."

The *Higher Self* is the part of our being that connects the earthly portions of consciousness with higher levels of consciousness. This is the level with relative unity of time and space, which is free from the emotions and thoughts of earthly reality. It remains untouched by what happens to us in our earthly existence.

It includes the comprehensive view of the life plan and the connection to the higher levels of consciousness such as the angels or Ascended Masters. The Higher Self is also the mediator between earthly life and the divine source. Its task is to support us during our life on this earth so that we live through all the learning tasks and experiences that we have planned for this life.

Waking consciousness, the unconscious mind, and the Higher Self are *individual*, which means they belong to a single person.

The *higher levels of consciousness* are closer to the divine source and therefore free of the laws of duality, valuations, judgements, and fear. The entities of the higher levels of consciousness exist in love and sympathize with a person's life and development on the basis of this love.

In addition to the higher levels of consciousness, which are sometimes also termed the causal level, there is the astral level. The beings of the astral level are still involved with earthly life, with fear and valuations, and are attached to the duality and the laws of cause and effect. This is where the souls of the departed belong, for example.

How the Higher Self Gives Us Support

Before we were incarnated on earth, we had selected the learning steps and experiences for ourselves for the next life. We bring along the potentials for this purpose. Each of us has enough strength and abilities to achieve everything that we have intended for ourselves.

After birth, we usually increasingly lose the connection with our higher consciousness aspect. Examples of this are given in the section on "Causes of Disorders and Blocks in the Energy System." In order for us to complete the pending learning steps despite these blocks, our Higher Self controls the events that make this possible. Among these are also the encounter with people who help us and with diseases. The Higher Self attempts to make us aware of our life plan and alert us when we deviate from it. If we follow this guidance and accept the learning tasks, we are content with our lives and expand our consciousness. If we don't follow these impulses because of restrictive beliefs ("I can't do this") or experiences ("My father couldn't do it either") that block us, for example, events in life will occur that are increasingly clear and easy to recognize as directions that lead us to this task. The inner tension increases until we ultimately look at this theme and become concerned with it.

Here is an example to illustrate this point: A person has intended to learn the theme of "accepting and living one's own strength." Already during his childhood days, in which he's very wild and boisterous, his parents constantly hold him back. The sentence "don't be so wild" is imprinted onto him. As a result, things often happen when he's wild and boisterous: he tips over a vase, breaks his arm while fighting, and has a car accident because he was driving too fast. Through these incidents he creates experiences and blocks that cause him to more intensively confront this theme.

If he increasingly subdues his strength as a reaction to these experiences, avoids all the situations in which he can react with full power, subordinates himself to others, and sees himself as a helpless and powerless victim of fate and the "evil world," he then avoids the learning theme. He doesn't learn. However, since he has planned to succeed at this task, the indications will become increasingly clear, the pressure that encourages or ultimately forces him to recognize and live his strength will become stronger and stronger. It may then happen that he chooses a partner in life who oppresses him and in whom he can see what it means to live out one's strength. This partner can constrict him to the point that he one day feels compelled to use his strength in a destructive fit of anger.

Another possibility for him to learn this theme would be lifting weights and practicing martial arts. There he can experience how his strength develops more and more and he can go beyond his limitations. He can then translate this experience to his life and also live out his strength there.

The Higher Self helps us create situations in life that make the pending learning experiences possible. It remains in harmony with the cosmic whole, receiving energy and impulses from it. When we have a good connection with our Higher Self, we use our intuition and life is easy for us. We have a sense of well-being and are content. Still, things will happen that we don't consider pleasant since these are connected with the learning steps. However, they no longer oppress us. Instead, we consider them to be fascinating challenges and welcome tasks.

The Path to Harmony

Every person has a waking consciousness, an unconscious mind, and a Higher Self. They belong together. Each part has its tasks, none of them are better or more elevated than the others. The goal is that all three work together to harmoniously shape life. The components of eating and drinking are just as important in life as an inner sense of well-being and harmony with the life plan. And both our logical minds and our creativity and intuition are parts that should be lived out.

Achieving the harmony between the different aspects is part of spiritual development.

If a person intensely or solely identifies with the waking consciousness, possessing a strong ego, he accepts very little information or few impulses from his unconscious mind. The contents of the unconscious mind trigger fear within him because they are foreign to him. The more he frees himself from the limitations and blocks, the more he will live in harmony with all three parts. This increases the permeability between the levels. Information from the higher levels of consciousness can then penetrate into the waking consciousness and be consciously perceived.

Spiritual development is called consciousness expansion or development since the borders between the individual levels increasingly dissolve. The permeability increases more and more until there ultimately is no more separation. All unconscious aspects become conscious, and light penetrates the darkness. When the borders have fallen completely, all the parts once again become a whole. The individual then merges with the cosmic consciousness, self-awareness is set aside, "the ego dies," and the drop once again unites with the cosmic ocean. This event is called enlightenment.

Part 2

The Work with the
LightBeings Master Essences

Chapter 4

The Effect of the LightBeings Master Essences

The LightBeings Master Essences can cause blocks in the energy system to resonate so strongly that they dissolve. This makes a harmonious flow of energy possible, and we live in increasing harmony with our true self.

Energy makes it possible for the body to transmit and process information. Information from inside and outside of the organism are in a constant state of flow within the human body. We receive impulses from the surrounding world, like the moods in the room or other people's emanations. Every part of the body within the organism is informed about the state of the entire body. This flow of information is the basis for the reactions and cooperation within the entire organism and for the work of control systems like the hormonal glands. Disorders in the flow of energy and information impair the balanced order (according to Köhler).

Adding information energy and work energy from the outside is possible. The result is bringing the work of the organism and the flow of energy in the subtle energy system back into equilibrium.

The term "in-FORM-ation" is Latin and means giving form to or shaping something. This suggests that an information belongs to every structure or form of material—and the other way around as well: every information influences the form and therefore the matter. Information itself is immaterial and takes the form of a vibration. Each vibration also simultaneously represents information that can change matter in some way (according to Köhler).

The LightBeings Master Essences contain energy impulses and information on the fundamental life themes or soul qualities. When an essence is used, the body and subtle systems receive impulses and resonance is created. As a result, the disorders are dissolved. When the impulses of the essence take effect for a longer period of time, the human being can once again enter into his natural vibrational frequency.

This picture can illustrate the effect: When there is a violin in a room and a tuning fork is struck, the violin produces a sound. When the tuning fork gives off a G note, the G string on the violin also begins to vibrate and the sound becomes audible. The other strings of the violin remain still. If the violin has no G string, nothing vibrates. There is no sound even though the tone of the tuning fork is in the room.

You can image a block to be a piece of wood on the G string of the violin. Even if the string is plucked, it can hardly vibrate and the sound can barely be heard, if at all. However, if the impulse is strong enough, the piece of wood vibrates so intensely that it falls off the violin.

Let's transfer this model to the model of the aura. If there is a disorder (corresponding with the piece of wood in the violin example) in a layer of the aura or in a G vibration, the G tone is either not transmitted at all or incorrectly transmitted. If the disorder is on the mental level, an oppressive thought arises. The corresponding places in the emotional body, in the ethereal body, and in the physical body are impaired by the falsely transmitted vibrational pattern. However, this isn't visible at first. After some time, a "piece of wood" is also found on the corresponding places in the emotional body, and still later, a symptom occurs within the body.

If the LightBeings Master Essence is used that contains the "G tone" in an intensified, pure form, the "G string" of the aura receives a strong impulse and therefore starts to vibrate so intensely that the block is dissolved (the piece of wood falls off). Afterwards, the other aura layers, which were cut off from the flow of energy before, also receive increasingly more energy. The system regulates and heals itself. A harmonization spreads on all levels like the domino effect: the first domino of an entire series of standing dominos is knocked down and the rest also fall as a result. If the disorder is healed, which means the aspect is balanced or lived out, the vibration is accepted and passed on in a pure state. All layers of the aura are permeable for the G vibration in an unrestricted manner.

Here is one example of this: An individual is burdened by his work, yet is unwilling to change something about it. An inner dialog may take place in which the two sides of "I don't want to do this anymore" and "but I have to, there's no other way" wrestle with each other (disorder in the mental body). After a while, he has a sense of unwellness when he starts his work (disorder in the emotional body), and ultimately comes down with a cold—he's fed up with things. Now he is "entitled" to withdraw and doesn't have to face the challenges. And he receives sympathy and understanding from the others, which he probably wouldn't have gotten had he just reduced his work load.

If he takes the corresponding Master Essences, he becomes aware of the conflict and searches for ways of improving his situation through things like delegation of work or through more effective planning.

Let's take a look at this effect using the example of the learning task "accepting and living one's own strength" from "The Lifework" in Chapter 3. The person described there has a block in relation to this theme. In situations in which he actually wants to react strongly and shape his life on his own, he draws back. He lets things take their course and feels himself to be a helpless, powerless victim. "I can't do it" is something he often says.

If he takes the Master Essence No. 6—*Djwal Khul*, he perceives that he has blocked his own strength. By not taking action, he has made himself into a helpless victim. He becomes aware of his limiting beliefs like "I don't have enough strength" or "others can do it better, there's no way I can do it" or he remembers situations from his childhood in which his strength and vitality were held back. The blocks start to dissolve, the energy related to the theme of strength begins to flow again, and he can work on trying out his strength and increasingly live it.

This example is the ideal situation. When the blocks are dissolved, it may be that an individual initially goes to the other extreme. You will find this extreme reaction partially described in Part 3 "Description of the 21 Master Energies" in the respective sections "A person who hasn't yet balanced this aspect."

In our example it may happen that as a result of the dissolved block the previously suppressed anger and feelings from the past once again become conscious. The person senses the tendency of demonstrating his strength and power to others, oppressing other people and avenging himself on them. Yet, at the same time he is capable of perceiving that these feelings and thoughts deal with his past and he has the choice of deciding what he does. He can recognize what it means to live his strength. He sees that keeping one's own strength in balance doesn't mean being rigid and that being in balance doesn't mean having to react immediately. Instead, it means acting in a way appropriate to the situation. Sometimes he will use his strength, and at other times he will do nothing. He can now freely decide what he will do—in contrast to how he was imprisoned in his pattern of behavior before this.

He can support and accelerate the transformational process by taking a precise look at things and becoming aware of old patterns through methods like meditation or writing lists (see section on "Techniques for Supporting the Process of Becoming Conscious" further down in this chapter. A conversation with a competent person is often helpful as well.

At the moment that the Master Essences give the impulse on the theme "accepting his strength," it may also be that this person initially goes even more intensely into his role as victim on the basis of his inner resistance. The limiting beliefs, his condemnations on the theme of "strength" and the fixed behavior patterns have such a strong effect that extreme emotions and physical reactions result. It may be that the person "can't get any air" because deep breathing connects him with his strength. Flat breathing blocks his strength. If he continues to take the Master Essences, he will become aware of this correlation and open up to his strength. Therefore it's important to continue to use the Master Essences until stability has been achieved. During the period of strong reactions, no fundamental decisions regarding life should be made.

It also may be that this person experiences what it means to "live his strength" through the impulse of the essence. He feels powerful, is in his center, self-confident, self-secure, and appears to be even-tempered. This gives him a taste of where he wants to go.

After a while, he will fall back out of this state. However, he can recognize what has previously hindered him from living like this and why he has returned to the old ways of behaving. On the basis of his own experience, he now knows how he could live if he succeeds in removing the blocks that let the collected experience become everyday life.

The blocks dissolve only to the degree in which someone consciously and unconsciously is willing for them to do so. The process of becoming healed can be supported by thankfully accepting the reactions and insights and through the techniques for becoming conscious described further down in this chapter.

The strength of the emotional or physical reaction is dependent on the learning theme. If this is a central issue in relation to which we have had many oppressive experiences and blocks, the inner resistance is stronger and we tend to have more vehement reactions. The process could have been easier and more pleasant for the person described had he initially used No. 3—*El Morya* "Trust." This Master Essence would have intensified the trust in himself, in his own strength and his path in life. As a result, the resistance is diminished and he has a foundation for more easily accepting his strength. He has trust in his strength and in the process.

Because of this, we recommend in the section on "The Selection" that the "right" question be asked when choosing the essences. Don't ask: "What Master Essence brings me in contact with my life theme?" or "What essence will help me make the quickest progress?" but: "What Master Essence will lovingly support me in a pleasant way and strengthen me at this time?"

If our person takes the Master Essence No. 6 for a period of time, he will come into balance with the theme of "accepting his strength." He lives his strength without having to demonstrate it to the outside world and acts on the basis of inner strength. After a while, he will feel that he has concluded with this theme for the time being and a new theme has now come up. Or he forgets to take the Master Essence.

It's possible that the theme of "strength" returns as a learning step, but this will be on another level. We develop in steps. We perceive the deeper limitations step-by-step and then purify what we might call the next layer.

Through subtle vibrations, the body's disorders can be healed. However, this doesn't occur as a result of the Master Essence directly affecting the body and its organs, but through a balancing of the energy flow between the energy bodies, chakras and meridians, the physical body, and the Higher Self. The learning step is taken, and the original purpose of the disease becomes irrelevant. The disorders begin to dissolve, and the energy flows harmoniously once again. The body begins to heal itself.

This harmonization of the energy flow and the process of becoming conscious can prevent physical diseases because the theme has been worked through and integrated on a mental and spiritual level. As a result, support is also given to any specialized treatment. The Master Essences are neither a therapy nor a remedy in the sense of orthodox medicine. They don't replace any type of medical or psychological treatment or medications that may be necessary.

During the healing process, causes like bottled-up emotions or impeding beliefs once again come into consciousness so that we live through the same feelings and thoughts one more time or encounter them in our surroundings. We can then see the pattern and ways of behaving in other people or come into situations that deal with the corresponding theme. It may be that we react in an irritated, tired, or restless manner. Physical symptoms that we have experienced at an earlier time may also appear again. The body reacts with detoxification or purification processes. This is why it's important to drink plenty of water (two to three liters daily) during the first days of application so that the dissolved toxins can be eliminated.

After a transitional phase, we have more energy at our disposal. We feel powerful, balanced, joyful, more free and clear. We increasingly achieve the state of our true being on all levels. This process is comparable with a spiral that winds upwards.

LightBeings Master Essences and Spiritual Development

Through the impulses of the Master Essences, the body's energy system begins to vibrate at a higher frequency. As a result, these impulses also open and strengthen the connection with the Higher Self. We find easier ways of perceiving, living, and achieving our purpose in life.

Spiritual development leads us to greater conscious perception of the totality, God, or the divine. We experience ourselves as part of the unity and increasingly understand the correlations and effective framework in our life, on the earth, and in the cosmic totality. The unconscious aspects of our being decrease, as if a dark room were slowly being illuminated. Perhaps this is also the origin of the term "enlightened one" for people who have achieved this state of consciousness. We perceive that we ourselves are "our life's master" and assume responsibility for our entire life along with everything that happens in it.

Reactions to the Master Essences

What Changes?

People react in a great variety of ways to the LightBeings Master Essences. Frequently, very sensitive people even feel the vibration of the bottles from far away. Some people have told us that they were passing a store in which the essences were sold and felt themselves drawn to it. They entered the store without knowing what they actually wanted and purposefully went to the bottles.

People with psychic abilities often perceive the effect through the closed bottles. When taking the tincture or applying the oil, they feel the reaction in their energy field as an intensified flow of energy, change in the emotions, and an expansion of the aura, or even a transformation in their thoughts. Those who are able to see auras can observe changes in the aura, which become visible for everyone through Kirlian photography.

The use of the essences triggers mental, emotional, physical, and spiritual reactions, as already described in the chapter on "The Effect." As a result, things that are old, suppressed, and perhaps undesired can also be brought to consciousness again. This detoxification process can appear in our moods, feelings, thoughts, dreams, or even our physical body as well. For some people, the toxins are increasingly eliminated through the skin and the smell of their perspiration may change.

In addition to the old things that become conscious, themes that an individual is currently suppressing may come up as well:

decisions that should be made but are put off; situations with which a person is dissatisfied, yet still overlooks and considers tolerable because of fear of a confrontation, for example; or wishes and visions that someone doesn't permit himself to have.

Don't be surprised if you dream more than you normally do since this is a possibility for the body to process experiences. And this also happens when you've forgotten your dreams. As Peter Mandel (healing practitioner and founder of color-acupuncture) says: "Dreaming is the bowel movement of the soul!"

It may be that experiences from the past come up. You may have the impression that you require support in facing them or feel yourself overwhelmed in dealing with them on your own. In these cases, we advise you to look around for a qualified therapist.

Through the use of the essences, a restructuring takes place on many levels that may temporarily result in the feeling of insecurity, difficulty in making decisions, a sense of perplexity, fluctuations in feelings, reduced initiative, and greater emotional vulnerability until the new structure has been created. Sometimes feelings of great joy and euphoria or hopelessness and sadness also appear at the beginning of the application. In such states, we tend to see our life circumstances in a way that is unrealistic, either too negatively or too positively. For this reason, you should make a pact with yourself not to implement any greater changes or make any hasty decisions in your life during this initial period.

Once the new structures have been created, you will have more clarity, stability, joy in life, and farsightedness. As a result, the further steps can be better planned.

Other people apparently don't experience anything. However, after continual use they determine that there have been changes within themselves after some weeks or months. An example of this may be that they are more open, stable, balanced, self-confident, and simply have become "more themselves."

As a reaction to the essences, people also notice thoughts that they hadn't had before. They make decisions in everyday life that they hadn't considered it possible a short time before. Old patterns of behavior that have accompanied them for a long time suddenly disappear without the individual being able to put a finger on when this change actually happened. Sometimes people don't even notice the occurring changes because they have taken place in such a slow and natural way. Only in retrospect, as a result of writing a journal or feedback from acquaintances, do they recognize their own development.

The reactions to the dissolution of blocks, as already described, can also be greatly varied. People who have the expectation that spiritual development is associated with suffering, drama, and catharsis often have more vehement reactions. They may experience mood fluctuations, weighty dreams, as well as impressive events that are related to the theme of the essences.

The effect and intensity of the reaction is related to a person's own attitude, willingness, and openness. Those who consciously invite the vibrations into their aura will achieve the strongest effects. Excessive strain is also avoided if you begin with the Master Essences that strengthens and supports you at the moment (see section on "The Right Question for the Choice").

The Outer World Also Reacts

During this stage, the reaction of the surrounding world should also be taken into consideration. This is particularly important in the area of relationships. Every change within one of the partners sets something into motion in the relationship. If both people are on the "path of growth," they will have more understanding for each other. Both partners are then familiar with reactions to the "growth steps" on the basis of their own experiences and are more willing to be tolerant. If just one of the partners within a relationship is "on the path," this may result in a tense situation. The changes are then found to be threatening, fears of loss arise, and the question about the meaning in life (which had been successfully suppressed for the other partner up to this point) is no longer so easy to overlook. The reaction is often a lack of understanding, the practical question of "What are you going to do now?," or even anger and irritation. The "old peace and quiet" and apparent "harmony" now begins to falter.

To make matters worse, there is sometimes the additional factor of women tending to have more emotional reactions and men having more practical ones. Women describe their emotions and feel themselves misunderstood when men ask: "Why is this happening now? What should we do? What can I do?" Men often have a difficult time comprehending emotional outbursts and feel that they are helpless.

As already mentioned, some people experience intense emotional reactions and unrealistic states as a result of working with the Master Essences. Under these circumstances, it may be easy to throw something overboard that will later be regretted—"throwing out the baby with the bathwater," so to speak. This should be taken into consideration when working with the Master Essences.

Perhaps it may be helpful to tell the partner what's happening inside of you at the moment and ask for understanding and patience. Once his attitude that *he* must help right now, that *he* must find the solution to the problem, or that *he* is the one who "does everything wrong and is to blame" changes, he can learn to observe and accept the process. If he also feels himself accepted in his situation with his fears and problems, it will give him support as well. Asking how he feels about things could help him relax. However, the partner shouldn't be put under any pressure.

The relationship with the partner and the surrounding world is a part of our path, helping us to learn and respect the connection with all being and treat each other with love. Perhaps this is even the most difficult area because things become concrete here—an individual's own standpoint is directly reflected and becomes visible in the outside world.

Chapter 5

Using the Essences

There are a total of 21 LightBeings Master Essences, each available as an oil, a tincture, and a Master-Energy ball.

The Selection

LightBeings Master Essences can be selected according to several different aspects:

The Momentary Themes in Life

You can do work on life themes and soul qualities with the Light-Beings Master Essences. You can choose the essence according to the momentary theme or a theme that repeatedly comes up in your life. The key words given in the description of the individual Master Essences ("A person who hasn't yet balanced this aspect ...") in Part 3 can simplify the choice.

When using this method, you should take into consideration that you will often select completely different themes on the basis of the rational mind than from your unconscious. We are often blind to our own problems and their causes. If we weren't blind at this point but could see what we lack, the symptoms wouldn't have occurred.

In addition, our rational mind often makes a selection in accordance with the state that we want to achieve and overlooks the steps between. This makes the path more difficult. If you wear size 16 and want to achieve size 12 with a diet, it may be that your wishful thinking causes you to buy an article of clothing in size 12 the next time you go shopping. However, you will have a hard time getting into it.

The Master-Energy Cards

As in Tarot, you can use cards to find the appropriate Master Essence for your theme (LightBeings Card Set). Ask your question. For example, this could be: "What essence strengthens and supports me in a loving way at the moment? Keep your question in your conscious mind while you draw the card. In doing this, your hand will be attracted by the energy of the card and the master energy connected with it. This procedure is based on the interplay between the unconscious mind and the Higher Self.

Test

You can also use other test procedures such as the pendulum, the biotensor, or the kinesiological muscle test.

You will find a *pendulum table*, which can be enlarged for work with the pendulum, in the Appendix.

The *kinesiological muscle test* is done in the following way: The person who is being tested (called "testperson" in the following) drinks a sip of water before the test. Then he lifts his left or right arm and stretches it to the front or side at a right angle. The person doing the testing (called the "tester" in the following) stands next to the testperson and places one hand on the shoulder and the other above the wrist. Then the tester asks the body to give a clear signal for "yes" and says "remember it." The testperson tries to hold the arm in the horizontal position while the tester attempts to push it downwards. Then the tester asks the body to give a signal for "no," again says "remember it," and pushes the arm downwards. The stretched arm usually offers a distinctly greater amount of resistance for "yes" and lets it be pressed down much more easily for "no." It may also be the other way around in some cases.

The various essences can then be tested. The best way to do this is for the testperson to take the essence in his hand and place it on his sternum (the middle of the chest).

Afterwards, the tester asks: "Is this the essence that is the right one now and that supports and strengthens (*name of test-person*)?"

If a greater number of questions are asked, it's important to always take a little break after three or four questions to prevent signs of fatigue.

The muscle test described here is a traditional test. Experienced kinesiologists use other testing procedures. This form is the easiest for beginners, although the arm tires quickly.

Intuition

You can naturally also let yourself be guided by your intuition. Or you can slowly move your hand over the bottles and sense which one you feel drawn to.

Can the Wrong Essence Be Selected?

Each essence always has an effect. This also applies to essences that don't work on your momentary "bottleneck." It therefore isn't possible to choose a "wrong" essence. However, one essence can prove to initiate stronger changes than another.

We have strong blocks or a lesser flow of energy in relation to some of the themes, while we live out others quite well. The developed or blocked themes are different for every individual. When we support the development of a life theme by working with the corresponding Master Essence, another theme becomes the bottleneck after a period of time.

The illustration on page 61 is meant to illustrate this somewhat by using the example of a cup. The rim of the cup represents the energy flow. If this is complete and evenly high, we have fully developed our potential and live our true existence. A block or a bottleneck in one quality of life is depicted as a nick in the cup, from which a liquid (our energy) leaks out. The numbers symbolize the learning themes according to the associated essences.

Let's once again use the theme of Essence No. 6—"accepting one's own strength"—as our example. This theme is most intensively blocked in the illustration (the rim of the cup is lowest here). When a person has worked with the Master Essence No. 6 for a time, he can live a more energy-charged and fulfilled life (the column is higher, the cup can become fuller). "Trust" is now the theme of the bottleneck or the theme in which his energy leaks out. We recommend that he continue working with the Master Essence No. 3 *El Morya*.

Even the essences that don't work on the current bottleneck are effective. No. 3 *El Morya* therefore increases the trust (the rim of the cup is raised with No. 3), yet the effect of No. 3 can't be as distinctly perceived as would be the case with No. 6. The theme of No. 6—"accepting your own strength"—remains the bottleneck. The energy still leaks out at this theme.

If this theme is worked on right after the theme of "trust," this may be more pleasant since the entire system has become more stable as a result.

Based on this context, there are two fundamentally different procedures for using the essences:

- Follow the order from No. 1 to No. 21. This means that each life theme is worked on independent of its priority.
- Work with a "bottleneck orientation" and choose the essence that is right at the moment or that you select on the basis of a testing procedure.

The decision of whether to use the tincture, oil, or Master-Energy Ball can also be tested with the methods described above.

The Right Question for the Choice

Which essence you select naturally also depends on your question. If you request an essence for your life theme, you will probably receive a different answer than if you ask for an essence related to your momentary situation or for strengthening in a current problem theme. This is why you should first decide what type of support you need from the essence.

It also makes a difference if you ask: "Which master energy will help me progress the farthest at the moment?" or "What master energy will strengthen me now in a pleasant way?" The

Portrayal of the bottleneck principle using the example of a cup

essence that will most greatly accelerate your development can possibly create the most vehement reactions.

The Tincture

The tincture as a water-alcohol mixture spreads very quickly in the aura bodies through the easily volatile alcohol. Its vibration can be perceived immediately after taking it, and its effects are primarily in the mental area. On the basis of its quick effect and easy handling, the tincture can be taken at any time when a person has the feeling that he needs support.

The Oil

The oil has a stronger effect in the areas that are emotional, physical, and close to the body. It needs some time before it spreads in the body and in the subtle aura layers. Oil is difficult

63

to use in some situations, such as while traveling (oil spots on clothing).

The Master Essence oils contain a mixture of various basic and essential oils. Since we don't use any emulsifiers or preservatives, it may happen that the oils separate. This means that the essential oils may stand out as streaks or flakes. They can be homogenized again by giving the bottle a firm shaking. Streaks don't impair the energetic effects.

The oil shouldn't be stored in the sun or in very warm places since this may influence its smell. However, the energetic effects remain unchanged.

If you don't like the smell of an oil, you can take the corresponding tincture.

The Master-Energy Ball

Because of its permanent effects, the Master-Energy Ball should be selected according to a theme that you want to work on intensively. We also recommend that you use the methods described above to make your choice for this purpose. Before you start working with a Master-Energy Ball, you should have first used an essence as an oil or tincture for a few days. Your body will have adapted to the work with the master energy, and less tensions will result. The Master-Energy Balls are effective throughout the higher spiritual aura layers and connect very strongly with the Higher Self and the level of the master energy in particular. Impulses from there then continue down into the physical level.

How to Use the Essences

You will receive the strongest effect if you use the Master Essences in a very conscious way. Make sure that you are clear about the theme of the essence before you take the tincture or apply the oil and invite the energy to harmoniously support you. After you have taken the essence, applied the oil, held the ball in your hand, or hung the ball around your neck, be silent for a while and pay attention to what happens. While doing this, you can focus your eyes on your breathing, on how your body feels, on your emotions, thoughts, inner images, and sounds.

It can be very helpful if you create a ritual for using the essences such as: take the bottle in your hands and become very still. Consciously make contact with the theme and open yourself for new perceptions. Then apply the essence and perceive how the vibration spreads throughout your entire body and into all the aura layers. Observe the reaction. In closing, thank your body, your unconscious mind, and your Higher Self for their support.

You can also strengthen the effect if you read the description of the respective energy and pay attention during the course of the day to inner and outer experiences related to the themes mentioned.

Bottles or Master-Energy Balls that you have already used can be given to other people because all of the products are energetically sealed. This means that they don't take on foreign energy from the outside.

The essences are ready to use and shouldn't be diluted since this clearly reduces their effectiveness.

You should definitely drink large quantities (two to three liters daily) of water or herbal tea when you use the essences in order to support the body's detoxification processes. Coffee, black tea, and alcohol aren't supportive drinks. On the contrary—when you drink them, you should consume additional liquids since coffee and black tea deprive the body of water.

A Note on Shelf Life:
The energy vibration in the essences is also completely effective after the expiration of the shelf-life date. The shelf life refers to the water and the oil. The smell of the oil may be impaired—particularly when the storage temperature is too warm—but the energetic effect remains.

The essences shouldn't be stored on or close to strongly radiating electrical equipment (television, washer, microwave, etc.).

Using the Tincture

Place one to two drops respectively of the tincture under your tongue, at best in the morning directly after getting up and in the evening before going to sleep. *Exception:* No. 10—*Kamakura* energizes and should therefore only be used in the morning or during the day. The essences have a stronger effect if you additionally take the tincture several times during the day.

The tincture can also be rubbed into the palms of the hands and fanned through the aura or applied directly to the skin. In this way, the tinctures can also be effectively used in working with others.

The tincture's effect lasts for several hours.

Using the Oil

Apply a few drops of oil to the recommended spots (see section on "Description of the 21 Master Energies"). It's basically beneficial to put it on:

- The pulse on the wrist since many meridians run along here.
- The seventh cervical vertebra—the seventh cervical vertebra is the one that protrudes the most along the cervical vertebra; this is also the entrance for cosmic energy.
- The lower end of the spinal column.

We also recommend that you rub it into other areas of the body where you have problems—naturally excluding open wounds or burn blisters.

The oil's effect lasts for several hours.

Using the Master-Energy Ball

The Master-Energy Ball can be worn on a chain like a piece of jewelry or placed on specific parts of the body. In comparison to the oil and the tincture, the energy ball has a continuous effect while it is worn. If the reaction is too strong at the start, then first wear the energy ball for a shorter period and take it off again in between times. Your body will adjust to the vibration after a certain amount of time, and you can then wear the ball constantly.

The Master-Energy Ball also has an effect even when you no longer perceive it. You will usually sense the difference when you have put the ball aside for a few days.

We were very surprised when some people informed us that the ball cracked without any external influence a short time after they had received it. They had placed the energy ball on the body and hadn't touched it afterwards. A short time later, the ball cracked. This also happened frequently when the ball was put on the navel.

The energy balls are made of a special glass that is approx. one millimeter thick. They are usually very stable and have survived a "test fall" from a height of 1.5 meters onto a stone floor.

Our explanation is that particularly at the beginning, the difference between the vibrational frequency of the ball and a person's own frequency is so great that the glass cracks because of the tension. Our recommendation: before you work with an energy ball, it's best to use the corresponding Master Essence for several days—preferably as a tincture—so that your energy system can adapt to the new vibration.

Other Possibilities

All Master Essences support meditation. For this purpose, you can hold the bottle or ball in your hand during the meditation or place it in front of you.

It's possible to combine different Master Essences. You can work on one theme with a tincture and on a second theme with an oil. A combination intensifies the effect, and the Master Essences can mutually support each other. Taking the tincture and the oil of the same Master Essence will intensify the effect of this energy.

However, you shouldn't use more than three different Master Essences at the same time. Otherwise, this may agitate too many things within you. Here is a comparison: If you have five pots on the stove that all need tending at the same time, it's very strenuous and you don't know where to start.

Just like the question of which essences to select, the amount of Master Essences should be chosen through a testing process.

The rational mind sometimes has a different opinion than the advice of our inner wisdom.

For What Period of Time Should the Essence Be Used?

There is no generally valid answer to this question. The length is dependent upon how strong the block or disharmony is, the theme's position in a person's path in life, the current learning step at the moment, and how quickly what has been learned is translated into action and integrated.

Once you have already used an essence, you will probably apply it again after a certain amount of time. This means that you subsequently work on the deeper areas of this aspect.

When you work on a certain theme, it's recommended that you use the essence for a number of days or weeks on a regular basis. If, after intensive work with the essences, you forget to use them or no longer have a desire to do so, this can be an indication that this theme has been completed for the time being.

You can gain many perceptions about your own process if you write a journal during the work with the Master Essences or think over the theme after its conclusion with the following questions:

- What changes have taken place in my life during this time?
- What attitude do I now have towards this theme?
- Have my behavior, my thinking, my feelings, or my sensations changed?
- What people do I now encounter?

After such a retrospect, we often determine what has happened and can further intensify the learning experiences as a result.

Techniques for Supporting the Process of Becoming Conscious

As previously mentioned, energetic blocks are dissolved through the work with the essences. This process can be supported by various methods like meditation. As a result, correlations become conscious that hadn't been perceived before. We advise you to deal with these experiences. Work with a method that you are familiar with and find to be effective or use one of the techniques listed below. These will help you more quickly work through the themes at hand.

On the basis of our practical experience, we have selected several methods that are easy to carry out and very effective:

- Writing lists
- Meditating with a candle
- Visualizing a purification of body and soul

You can naturally also use the meditations depicted in the description of the master energies. In this case, at the beginning of the meditation you should be aware of your momentary situation or request that the energy be used to heal it.

It's important to us that meditation is enjoyable. We therefore recommend that you select the technique that most appeals to you. If you meditate with enjoyment and happiness, you will do it with so much more energy and consciousness than when you force yourself to do it and your thoughts constantly drift away. Try out the described methods. However, after you have decided on one technique you should stay with it for a while and use it every day.

It's more effective to work on a theme and meditate for five minutes every day than to do so for half-an-hour once a week.

Writing Lists

First select a theme, such as the theme of the Master Essence with which you are working currently or one that is significant for you.

The themes for writing lists could be thoughts, feelings, words, or sentences with which you are frequently confronted in your momentary situation like trust, guilt, patience, or money. You can also use terms from the descriptions of the Master Essences that are emotive words for you.

Take a piece of paper and a pen. Sit down.

While you observe how your body and your aura fills with light, connect yourself with your unconscious mind and ask for its help.

Afterwards, take two minutes to write down everything that comes to mind in response to the question: "**What does** (insert the theme at this point) **mean for me**?"—no matter whether these are pleasant or oppressive thoughts or feelings.

Simply let the words and sentences flow. Don't put much thought into the process. It isn't important for the sentences and words to have a meaning or that they are written down clearly. Sometimes just keywords or even signs or words that you aren't familiar with may come. Follow the impulses—it doesn't have to be legible in the end.

In case you have difficulties at the beginning or nothing comes at first, simply write the theme down on paper a few times. After a period of time, words and sentences will then flow on their own.

When the two minutes are over, stop the list and write "**thank you**" beneath it.

You should really limit yourself to two minutes with this technique and write down your spontaneous thoughts. If you allow yourself more time, the rational mind will become too involved.

Then burn this list and ask your unconscious mind to let go of everything that is related to this theme and is willing to go away. Let this flow into the flames as well. The flames will transform the energy.

In closing, imagine how you once again take in the transformed strengthening energy. Then fill your body and aura with a color that heals you at this time.

Work on a theme with this method for eleven days. In case even more negative, oppressive sentences come up, extend this period by three days at a time. Write until only positive statements appear. Then you can start with the next theme.

You should "write lists" for at least eleven days, even if just positive, pleasant sentences appear after four days. In these cases, oppressive sentences from a deeper layer usually come up after a few days.

Some people have difficulty with burning the positive sentences of the list. If this applies to you, you can imagine that the positive things come true during the burning.

Meditating with a Candle

Create a calm atmosphere and sit down in front of a burning candle. Put all your thoughts, feelings, and everything oppressive into the flame of the candle. Perceive how these things become transformed and the healing light energy returns to you.

Purification Meditation

Assume a relaxed body posture and imagine how a stream of white light flows into your body through your crown chakra. Let the light slowly flow through your head, neck, arms and hands, the chest and stomach area, the back and lower belly, the legs and feet, and from there into the floor. You should let more light flow into problem zones. In the process, notice how the white light cleanses the entire body and transforms blocks. Afterwards, let the light flow through all the aura layers.

If it's easier for you to imagine feelings, feel how water with a pleasant temperature flows through you and cleanses you. You can also visualize purifying sounds.

What Is Meditation?

What do you imagine when you hear the word "meditation"?

Most people will see a person quietly sitting cross-legged (more precisely called the "lotus position") on a pillow with closed eyes and an attitude of silence. Inner tranquility is a desirable state, yet sitting still as a path is not the ideal way for everyone and certainly not the only way to find inner harmony.

The word "meditate" comes from Latin and means "going into the center"—and there are many different possible ways of doing this. The structured ways use techniques, such as sitting still, but also a series of motions (Gurdjieff dances, kundalini meditation with shaking and dancing), certain body positions or also the speaking of specific words, which are called mantras. These techniques make it easier to get away from the thoughts and go into the center, where a stillness of mind predominates. And it leads to experiences that are difficult to describe with words.

But meditation can also take place in everyday life when we come into our center and become aware of it through music, a walk in nature, or while dancing.

The LightBeings Master Essences support us in meditating and in coming into our center. As already described, you can also use them for meditation purposes and naturally also while talking a walk or dancing. This makes it possible to experience the meaning of the respective theme in a completely different way than with the rational mind.

Using the Master Essences for Other People

You can also use the LightBeings Master Essences to transfer the energy of the masters to other people. This is a transference of energy into the energy paths of the body and into various aura layers. In addition, disorders in the aura can be regulated through energy work.

In the following, the transference of energy to other people, sometimes also called treatment, is given the term *energy transference.* The person who transfers the energy is called the *giver,* and the person receiving the energy is called the *client.*

The energy of the masters can be included in every other type of application or treatment. You can use the methods described below as a technique. If you already transfer subtle energy with methods like therapeutic touch, Reiki, or prana healing, the energies of the masters can flow into these as well. You can then use the Master Essences in order to come into contact with the energy vibration of the masters.

The Master Essences are also effective in therapy forms like hypnosis, reincarnation therapy, and behavior therapy since they support the energetic aspect.

Every time you use them, it's important that you ground yourself!

If you are inexperienced, you will find a detailed description of possible energy transference with the Master Essences in the following: The more frequently you do this, the more practiced and secure you will become in their use. Don't let yourself be stopped by doubts and insecurities at the start. Doubts are normal for every human being. We also doubted our abilities at the beginning. When you try things out and practice, your confidence in yourself will grow. An additional factor is that you and the person receiving the energy will both be lovingly supported by the energies of the masters. If you should happen to feel insecure at some point, simply ask for help. In every situation in which I have requested help up to this day, I have also received support. I can therefore really encourage you to risk the step. *The most important thing is that you work from your heart, with compassion and love for others.* Be aware of this over and over again.

There are people who feel nothing when they start with the transference of energies. This applies to both the givers and the clients. Don't let this irritate you. The energies work despite this, and it's possible that you will become more sensitive for subtle energies after a certain period of practice and start to perceive them in your own way. This doesn't always have to be a feeling or a color. Some people see pictures, hear sounds and music, or perceive a fragrance during the application.

The Step-By-Step Transference of Energy

The transference of the master energy to others includes various steps that are extensively explained and illustrated in the following. As an orientation, here is a summary of the individual steps:

- Preparation
- Grounding yourself
- Establishing contact with the master energy
- Establishing contact with the client
- Smoothing out the aura
- Grounding the client
- Transferring the master energy to the body
- Working in the aura
- Smoothing out the aura
- Transferring the master energy into the chakra system
- Focusing attention
- Ending the energy flow
- Energy stroke
- Using the essences
- Cleansing

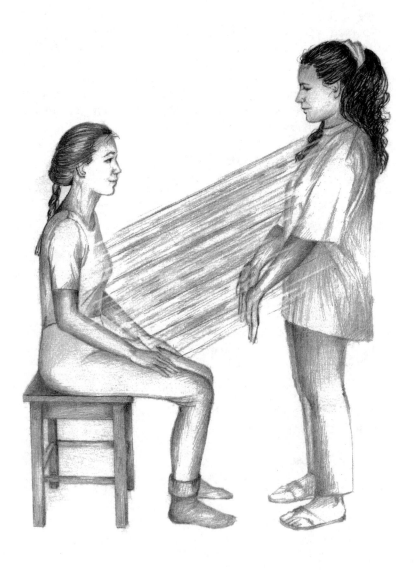

Establishing energetic contact and creating a heart connection

Preparation

The person who receives the Master Essence should sit down comfortably and select the appropriate essence. This can be done intuitively or with any type of test procedure. Be sure that the client poses the "correct" question when choosing the essence (see page 62). Sitting on a stool is best since this makes it easier for the giver to work on both the front and back of the client. It's important that neither the giver nor the client cross his arms or legs since this disturbs the energy flow. The client's arms can rest comfortably on his thighs, the feet should be next to each other and touch the floor with the entire soles.

It's also possible to transfer the essences to a person in a lying position. However, be sure that you can stand or sit comfortably while doing so. If the transference is unpleasant for you because your back is tense and you feel pain, you will stop enjoying it and the energy won't flow at full strength.

Grounding Yourself

Connection with the earth is very important in order to remain in your own center and be conscious in everything that happens. Without grounding, it may be that you drift or wander off into other dimensions, losing the contact and attentiveness to your client.

Ground yourself by consciously touching the floor with the entire soles of your feet and imagine that roots from your feet and the base of your spine are growing deep into the earth and branching out. Observe how the earth energy streams into your body through these roots.

Establishing Contact with the Master Energy

Before you apply the essence, relax yourself. To do this, go through your entire body with your consciousness and relax your head and face, particularly the eyes and the chin. The tip of the tongue can be gently placed on the upper gums. Relax your throat, neck, shoulders, and the spinal column, which also relaxes your back muscles. Then relax your arms, hands and fin-

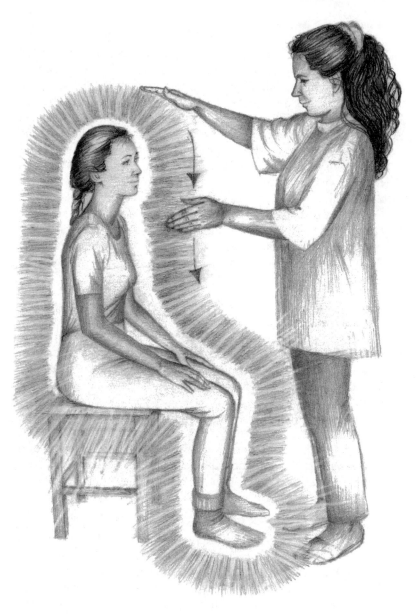

Smoothing out the aura

gers, chest, belly, stomach, abdomen, the muscles of your buttocks, your legs, feet and toes.

Spread the Master Essences on the palms of your hands and into your aura. Establish contact with the master energy and request support.

While you apply the essence as an oil or tincture, establish contact with the master energy. Imagine how this energy flows into your body through your crown chakra, into your heart chakra, and from there into your arms and hands. Then it flows back out through the palms of your hands and your fingertips. Move your hand two or three times through your own aura from top to bottom.

During the entire application, the master energy will stream through your crown chakra.

Establishing Contact with the Client

In order to establish energetic contact, hold the palms of your hands in the direction of the person. Then imagine how a cloud of light comes out of your heart chakra and envelops both of you. As a result, you will create an atmosphere in which you can work on the basis of compassion and love, without imposing your own will. You create a space in which the client has a feeling of wellness and acceptance and permits healing reactions.

Remain in the energy for a few minutes and attune yourself to it.

Consciously observe how the master energy flows through you. Request support for the transference and so that the energy has a supportive and strengthening effect on the client.

You can request the master energy to also work within you while you transfer it to the other person. However, you should check to be sure this isn't too much for you at the moment.

Smoothing Out the Aura

Position yourself behind the client and hold the palms of your hands in his direction.

Start the application on the back side because this isn't as intimate and usually more pleasant for the client. The palms of the hands are once again directed towards the client.

Smooth out the aura. Start at a distance of about 50 centimeters above the back of the head. As you approach the body, you will run into one or more layers, the transitions of which you can perceive. Some people sense the surface of an aura layer to be a condensation, like a pad of cotton, in the prickling or tingling in their hands, or as a type of heat or a cold breeze. Other simply know where the aura layer begins or ends without feeling anything.

Place your hands above the back of the head and start slowly smoothing out the aura from the head to the feet. Very sensitive people can perceive disorders in the form of holes, bulges, and resistance when they do this.

Smooth out the aura from the head to the feet, as if you were petting a cat's fur. Slowly walk around the person while you do this and smooth the aura from all sides.

Grounding the Client

You should also ground the client by placing your hands on his feet and imagining that roots are growing out of his feet into the earth as well. You can put your hands on the tops of the feet and/or on the soles of the feet while you do this.

Transferring the Master Energy to the Body

Place your hands on the shoulders and let the energy streaming out of your hands flow into them. At the same time, it's possible to get an impression of the client's state—whether he's tense or relaxed, fearful or energy-charged.

Then place your hands on the nape of the neck, followed by one hand on the forehead and the other on the medulla (at the back of the head where the spinal column makes a transition into the cranial bones). Afterwards, place one hand on the back of the neck and hold the other at a distance (about 10 to 30 centimeters) in front of the larynx. Be sure to stay at an adequate distance since most people are very sensitive in the throat area. At latest when you observe that your client is constantly swallowing should you notice that you are too close.

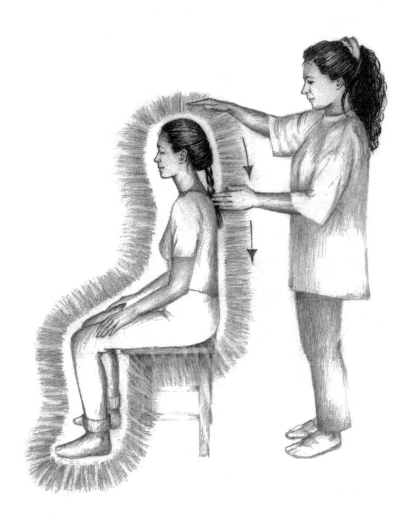

Energy transference to the aura

Then give the master energy to the left shoulder joint by placing one hand on the back side of the shoulder and the other on the front side. Use the same approach with the left elbow, the wrist, and finally hold the left hand between your hands. Repeat the same thing with the right shoulder and the right arm.

Afterwards, energize the chest area by placing one hand in the middle of the sternum (heart chakra) and the other on the opposite side between the shoulder blades. Then bring your hands to the back at the height of the kidneys (beneath the ribs). Afterwards, transfer the energy to the spinal column by placing one hand on the base of the spine and the other at the end of the cervical vertebra at the back of the head. While doing this, imagine how the energy flows between your hands along the spinal column.

Energy transference to the aura

Then change to the front and place your hands on the belly, the hips (between the ends of the ribs and the hipbones), the knees, the inner and outer ankles, and once again on the feet.

Hold each position for one-half to one minute.

If your client has complaints at certain points of the body, you should also supply these with energy and possibly stay there longer.

Working in the Aura

After the body has been charged with the master energy, start energizing the aura. Choose an aura layer and let your hands slowly glide from top to bottom through the aura. The palms of your hands face the client while you do this. Start on the back side once again at the height of the back of the head. Let yourself be guided by your hands, and fill the selected aura layer with energy, once again from the head to the feet. Then change to the person's front side and energize it in the same way.

If you would like, you can also supply a further aura layer with master energy. However, be sure to notice when this gets to be too much for your client. It's better for the first application that someone receives to be short. The more familiar the client

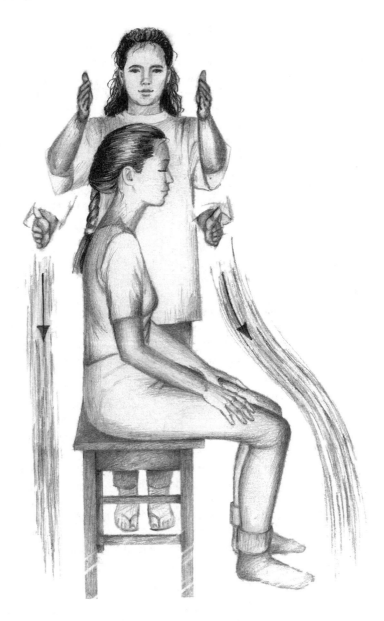

Transferring the master energy into the chakra system

is with the master energy, the more energy he will be able to accept. You can also request him to tell you when he has had enough or ask him during the treatment. You should additionally pay attention to your own feeling and trust your intuition. If you have the impression that enough energy has flowed, then end the session.

If the client feels dizzy or unwell, his energy system will have a hard time integrating the transferred energy. These feelings will once again disappear on their own after a time. You can support this by smoothing the excess energy down into the earth with your hands (as in the section on "Smoothing Out the Aura"). This state will usually improve within a short time thereafter.

Smoothing Out the Aura

You can stroke away the energetic blocks that were dissolved during the energization. Let your fingertips glide lightly over the body or through the client's aura and pull out these dissolved blocks as if you were raking together old dry leaves. Here you should also move from the head to the feet (like petting a cat's fur). Every time you reach the feet, shake out your hands just like you would shake the old dry leaves out of the rake.

Transferring the Master Energy into the Chakra System

After the aura has been cleansed and energized, let the master energy flow into the chakra system. Hold your hands above the top of the client's head with the palms of your hands facing each other. One hand is on the front side of the body, the other is on the back side. Then draw the energy from about 50 centimeters above the top of the head to the feet by slowly letting your hands glide downwards, one hand at the front and one hand at the back of the body. The client's body is between the two hands.

Figure-Eighting

At the conclusion, focus your attention on the client by *slowly and carefully* drawing a figure eight (infinity sign) in the aura with the palms of your hands. Here as well, you should start on

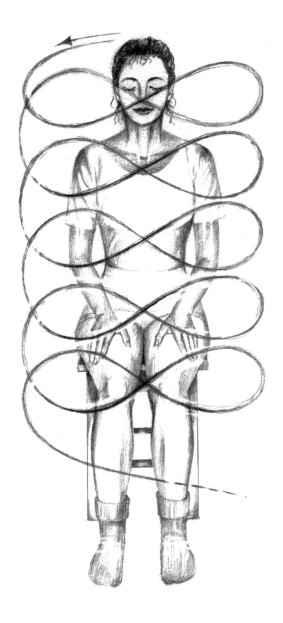

Figure-eighting

the back side at the level of the back of the head and slowly move down towards the feet. When you do this, you once again transfer harmonizing master energy into the aura.

Ending the Energy Flow

After the application, the influx of master energy stops when you take leave of it or ask the flow to cease. If you like, you can express gratitude for the support and the flow of energy.

Energy Stroke

By having his aura smoothed out and energy transferred to him, the client usually achieves a very deep state of relaxation. A stimulating effect is obtained when you stroke along the spinal column from the base of the spine to the head once or twice. Just like a cat becomes lively when you stroke its fur in the wrong direction, this also has an invigorating effect on human beings.

After Using the Essences

Give your client some time to come back into the present.

It may happen that a person sinks into a very deep state of relaxation and needs a while before he comes back into the here and now. Before the person leaves, make sure that he's completely awake and fit. This is particularly important if he wants to drive a car afterwards. You can talk with him for a while longer or encourage him to move his body. This is a good opportunity for connecting movement and the processing of what has just been experienced by having him dance to quiet music and express what he has experienced or his momentary state.

Cleansing

Flowing cold water has been used for energetic cleansing since time immemorial. In order to free yourself of everything that may be clinging to you, wash your hands under flowing cold water after completing the energy transference.

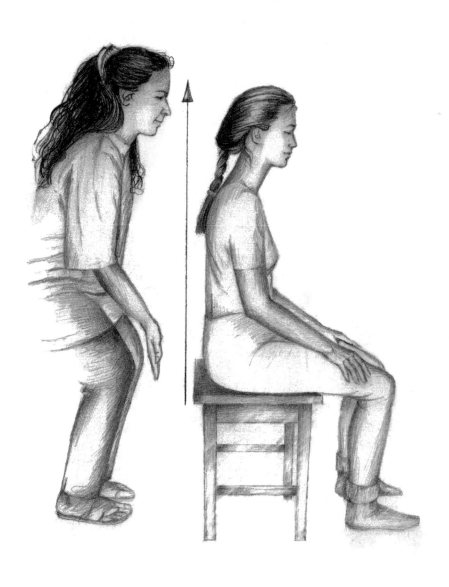

Energy stroke

Drink Plenty of Water

Processes are set in motion by the energy transference, and the body often starts a cleansing procedure. This applies to both the client and the giver. In order to support the body, both of you should drink plenty of water. As already mentioned, the effects of black tea or coffee are burdensome instead of a detoxifying.

Possible Client Reactions

Blocks begin to dissolve during the energy transference and the energy starts to flow again. The client may react to this in different ways. Some people feel strong emotions and start to laugh or cry; others sense heat or cold in the places where the blocks are; some may be very relaxed, calm and cheerful while others are discontent, sad, or don't feel well. However the client may react—these are signs of a change in the energy flow. If such a reaction occurs during the energy transference, let the energy continue to flow and carry on the process. In most cases, the client will relax again after a while. If the client begins to cry, give him a handkerchief and encourage him to let the tears flow. Tears cleanse, and much of the old tension is worked through as a result.

Using the Essences for Children

Childhood as a period of life is also part of the developmental path of consciousness and contains learning steps. After getting over illnesses, children have often taken mental and spiritual steps as well and become more "mature."

In addition, formative experiences are gathered during childhood and influence later life.

The connection between the Higher Self and earthly consciousness is often much more distinct in children than in adults. However, because of their socialization, through the conflict between what they experience themselves and what adults impart to them, the permeability between the levels is diminished.

The Master Essences let the divine core within a human being resonate. As a result, they can also support children in maintaining the natural harmony between the parts of being that are the Higher Self, the unconscious mind, and waking consciousness. And they help children go through their learning steps and grow in harmony with their life plan.

It's important that children decide on their own whether they want to use the Master Essences and that they also select these themselves!

We know parents who want to talk their children into using the Master Essences "because it would be good for the children, so that the children feel better as a result, or so that things will be much easier for the children," or by arguing that the oils "simply smell so good."

Usually children themselves know best what's good for them—particularly when it comes to things on the subtle level. They know exactly when they have had enough and when they need help. And there are some learning steps that they don't want to make easy for themselves but want to get through. When we, as caring parents, "know better" in respect to what is good for children, we convey to them that their own access, their own knowledge, their own inner truth is wrong. We may even destroy the access to and harmony with the Higher Self because we impart to the children that they themselves aren't capable of knowing what's right for them. This can lead to them increasingly turning to the outside world and listening to external "authorities" instead of their own inner voice.

If you would like to give support to children, offer them the Master Essences and leave the decision up to the individual child. The Master Essences should be used in the oil version for children since the tincture contains alcohol. Furthermore, the oil strengthens the connection of the subtle levels with the body, which is more similar to children's way of developing.

Suggestions for Therapists

The Master Essences support every form of therapy since they promote the process of becoming conscious. Clients therefore attain easier access to the meaning and reason for their illnesses or complaints, seeing through their own patterns of thought and behavior. They more quickly perceive what is truly involved.

Since we all know that the inner attitude has a large influence on the success of the therapy, physical symptoms are more quickly resolved when the mental learning step behind them has been taken and the purpose of the illness becomes irrelevant as a result.

The mental and spiritual principle of the Master Essences is also reflected on the physical level in the diseases. As an example: the Master Essence No. 4 "gets things flowing." If this principle is integrated in the mental area, bodily fluids that were previously congested on the physical level can now begin to flow and the detoxification processes are supported. No. 11 integrates "accepting one's physical nature" and thereby supports the functions of the body that increase vitality (breathing, blood circulation in the lower extremities).

The reactions that have already been described may naturally also occur on the way to healing. The therapist can give support and draw attention to the correlations between the mental and spiritual and physical area through clarity and in his role as the external observer and trusted counselor.

The therapist should keep an eye on "partnership" as a possible area of conflict (see section on "Reactions to the Master Essences," page 55). He should point out to the client that a person's own situation may be perceived unrealistically (too pessimistically or too euphorically) during the transitional phase.

The Master Essences can be applied supportively on a variety of levels in the work with clients. If the corresponding Master Essence is employed for a few days after the session, the therapeutic work will be intensified.

Mixing Tinctures

Tincture mixtures are possible as a further form of application. Above all, they are suitable for complete theme areas. There is a distinct difference in the effect, depending on whether you take one drop from a number of different tinctures or first mix them and then take the mixture. You can imagine the difference in the effect to be something like this: If you take a number of essences at the same time without mixing them, the individual energies are uncoordinated as they each work on their own theme area like workers who do their own jobs without discussing a cooperation. If you make one single mixture out of these same essences, the individual energies will form a team and coordinate their effects with each other.

Use your intuition to decide whether you would like to work with a mixture or with the individual essences.

Making the Mixture

Use the following process to do this:

1. Select the components of a mixture using the same process with which you usually choose the individual essences. This may be a card set, a biotensor, a pendulum, the muscle test, etc.

2. From each individual tincture, put a portion (for example, for four elements use the respective bottle contents) into an empty, clean glass bottle with a dropper or pipet stopper, close well, and shake a few times.

Important:

- As applies elsewhere, the tinctures should not be diluted to make the mixture.
- Use only bottles that close well, are either clean and new or have been rinsed with hot water or alcohol.
- Make only as much of the mixture as you can use in the next few weeks; for longer periods of time, it's better to make a new mixture when you need it.

The crisis-drops "RELAX" are a time-tested mixture. You can either make them yourself or purchase them in a ready-made form.

The LightBeings Master Essences "RELAX" Mixture

The LightBeings RELAX tincture is made of so-called "crisis drops" that can be employed for energetic conditions of shock caused by injuries or traumatic experiences.

People have had good experiences even against such small everyday states of indisposition like mosquito bites, skin injuries, headaches, etc. We always have RELAX on hand.

The RELAX Essence does not take the place of a doctor or naturopathic treatment!

The tincture strengthens, stabilizes, and harmonizes the body's energy flow, which can become unbalanced in crisis situations. With the RELAX Drops, the energy begins to flow again, a state of equilibrium is restored, and the body's self-healing powers are strengthened. The state of energetic shock can be overcome more quickly.

This essence also has the effect of clarifying the actual cause of the event and the learning steps behind it.

When you use it, you may relive old emotions.

Loving accept these reactions.

The RELAX drops can be combined with other LightBeings essences.

Composition of the RELAX mixture

No. 8—*Angelica*: Transforms the past and the causes behind the current incident; brings awareness of the causes and what we should learn from them; supports comprehension.

No. 9—*Orion*: Makes clear where we are at the moment, why the incident has occurred, and what step should be taken next.

No. 13—*Seraphis Bey*: Strengthens the entire energy flow (has a particularly strengthening effect on the hara and the first chakra), supports the body's powers of self-healing.

No. 18—*Lady Portia*: Brings us back into the state of inner equilibrium, which we have lost through the energetic shock; promotes inner peace and contentment.

No. 21—*Mary*: Strong energetic healing energy; healing on all levels.

Application

In crisis or shock situations, or for complaints, take several drops or apply externally (not onto open wounds or burns since it contains alcohol!), as needed. Apply a number of times, if necessary, every hour. It is also possible to put some drops into a glass of water and swallow slowly while drinking.

For children, it is best to use the tincture externally by putting several drops on the crown chakra. Otherwise, strongly dilute in water before giving it to them.

Part 3

Description
of the 21 Master Energies

Introduction

The energies and essences of the 21 masters are described in the following sections. The information given here applies both in general to the energy of the master with whom you work in meditation, for example, as well as for the LightBeings Master Essences.

All descriptions are structured in the same way:
- At the beginning you will find the *theme* through which the master energy can be developed.
- This is followed by a description of the *effect* of the LightBeings Master Essences.
- Then the *chakra* that is primarily effected by the essence is stated. Additional chakras that are also influenced are listed in parenthesis.
- *Colors, Tarot cards* (Rider Waite Tarot, the name in the Crowley Tarot in parenthesis), and *gemstones* are associated with the master energy. This classification makes it possible to more deeply understand the energy. In addition, colors and gemstones can be used together with the essences. An example of this is wearing the corresponding gemstone as jewelry.
- This is followed by the *parts of the body to which the oil can be specifically applied.* These recommendations were given to us by the masters. There is a drawing on the following page that explains them.
  As already mentioned, you can just apply the oil to your pulse and/or the 7th cervical vertebra or follow your intuition and rub it on the parts of the body to which you feel drawn with it.
- In conclusion is a portrayal of a *person who has balanced this aspect* or *has not balanced it*, which means has fully developed or blocked this soul quality. This description makes it easier to understand and select the right essence.

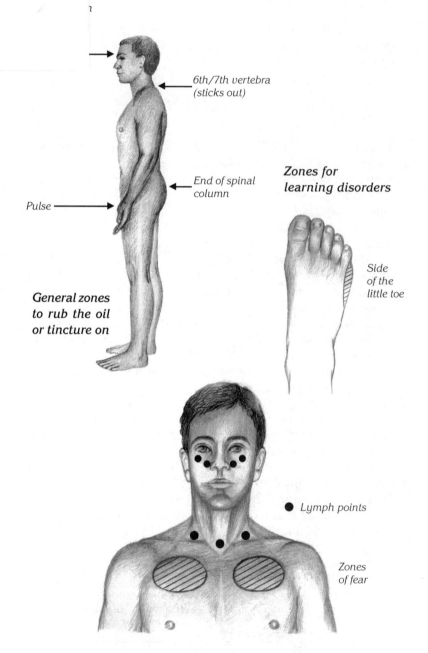

6th/7th vertebra
(sticks out)

End of spinal
column

Pulse

**General zones
to rub the oil
or tincture on**

**Zones for
learning disorders**

Side
of the
little toe

● Lymph points

Zones
of fear

Parts of the body for applying the oil or tincture

Remember that an extreme case is portrayed in the description in order to illuminate the condition. Not every point will apply to a single individual.

Sometimes there are overlapping statements in the depictions. The reason for this is that the same "symptoms" have varying causes and can also be remedied in different ways. An "inadequate sense of self-worth" can therefore come from being too strongly opinionated, for which No. 2—*Lao Tse*—is recommended. Or it may be because a person doesn't accept his own strength and sees himself as a victim. No. 6—*Djwal Khul*—is supportive in this case. The differences in the effect of the Master Essences for the same theme are briefly explained.

- Under the **description** section, some aspects of the effect are once again discussed and illustrated. Here you will also find the experiences of people who have used them.
- The **meditation description** has been given to us by the respective master. It represents a way of directly experiencing the energy of the master and the soul quality. In addition, it intensifies the effect of the essence.
- In closing, the channeled **message** of the master has been included.

No. 1—*Maha Chohan*

Inner Wisdom

The Effect of the Master Essence

The essence allows a person to inwardly take a step back and therefore observe his own actions. This makes it possible to clearly see and evaluate the situation. It therefore also helps in times of stress, when we have become engrossed in work, have lost control of things, and have dissipated our energies. Then it is possible to once again acquire a general idea of the situation, set priorities, and act according to our intentions.

It opens the contact to the unconscious mind and makes it easier to communicate with the inner and higher levels of consciousness. It makes it possible for us to hear the inner voice, the inner wisdom.

The essence helps us to understandably express perceptions because we have a general idea of our own position and include the standpoint of the person with whom we are talking.

Associated with the chakras: Throat chakra (forehead chakra)
Color: Turquoise
Tarot card: No. 5—The Hierophant (The High Priest)
Gemstone: Blue-Andes opal, green-blue tourmaline
Oil application: Throat and neck, forehead chakra

A person who has balanced this aspect:
- Can take an inner step back at any time.
- Maintains an overall view of things.
- Sees situations, people, and his own life with a sense of distance and in the right proportions.
- Is good at empathizing; has a very good grasp of the other person's state or the current situation and maintains his own standpoint at the same time.
- Meets other people where they're at, expresses himself understandably, and adapts to other people.
- Easily grasps processes, correlations, and interactions.

- Recognizes causes, backgrounds, and reasons from the position of a neutral observer who is capable of knowing all the aspects.
- Has a good contact with the unconscious mind, access to inner wisdom, and is open for impulses from the Higher Self and higher levels of consciousness.
- Brings "spirituality" into harmony with everyday life.
- Is capable of imparting wisdom and has teaching abilities.

A person who has not yet balanced this aspect:

- Easily gets tangled up in details; sees the world as if through a magnifying glass and thereby loses the general overview of things; "doesn't see the forest for the trees," things become too much for him and he's overwhelmed.
- Is so impressed by trivial things that he's inwardly occupied with them and isn't receptive to anything else from the outside world; is no longer responsive but caught up in his own world.
- Quickly loses the "red thread."
- Has excessive emotional reactions; stays stuck in feelings and is incapable of thinking clearly as a result.
- Has the sense of being "entangled and confused" and therefore feels constricted and constrained.
- Often makes the impression of losing his head and being without any orientation.
- Gets lost in trivial matters and details: "a stickler for details."
- Is imprisoned in his world and self-image; just sees his own world, doesn't perceive and accept impulses from the outside world; is opinionated.
- Is stuck in old patterns of behavior; one impulse is enough to let the pattern be played out again; doesn't learn from other people.
- Tends to generalize: everything, always, everyone, never....
- Is a very sensitive person who takes in more of his surroundings than others and more than he can process.
- Has difficulties in setting boundaries with other people; is often completely caught up in conversations with others, loses his own position, forgets his own feelings and needs.

- Is completely absorbed by other people; reacts strongly to the mood that's in the air.
- Has no access to the inner voice; therefore often has difficulties in making decisions because he can't see what's good for him in the long run.
- Has difficulties with stillness and meditation; as soon as he comes to rest, the images of the day runs through his head like a film; is so caught up in the events of the day that they continue in his thoughts.

But also a person who:
- Tends to be presumptuous and arrogant: "I know everything better, I know the right way to do it": the know-it-all.

A counselor who has not yet balanced this aspect:
- Suffers with the clients as a therapist; is trapped in their situations and stories; feels himself to be worn out, muddled, and confused after sessions; has a hard time drawing the line.
- As a counselor, interprets his own view of things, his own experiences, his own perspective of the world into the client and "advises" in a way that would be best for himself instead of seeing the other person's circumstances.
- Is often spellbound by the problems and opinions of his clients.

Description

Perhaps you remember how you learned to drive a car or ride a bike. While driving a car, you must keep an eye on the street, press the pedals with your feet, and also simultaneously operate the gear shift—so many things at the same time that a person loses the general overview of things and feels overwhelmed. There are also such situations in life. Everything appears important at the same time, and thoughts race through our minds. In this type of condition, access to inner wisdom and the inner voice is blocked.

The energy of *Maha Chohan* lets us step back a bit from the events of the day and look at them with a certain distance. It leads us into the role of the observer, in which we can both act and observe at the same time and understand the processes, correlations, and interactions. As a result of this distance, we can more easily overcome fears associated with the situation. We can recognize beliefs, examine and free ourselves from limiting thought structures and patterns of behavior. We see the things in the proper proportions and find our way back to our inner composure. Parts of the whole are no longer looked at with the magnifying glass.

A person who is entangled in the happenings of the day usually can't see any further than his own experiences. He judges other outlooks to be "false."

When we aren't caught up in the events around us, we can be open for suggestions and changes. We learn from people who deal differently with situations. Or we remember times in our own life when we have successfully mastered problems and difficulties. As a result, we find alternatives to the way in which we have behaved and acted up to now.

We use the image of a theater to illustrate the effect of *Maha Chohan*: the essence frees us from being bound up with our roles as actors. The actor who identifies with his role and believes that he is imprisoned in the role has no freedom of action. He only sees himself and his role and must act according to its dictates.

Through the essence, he goes into the auditorium and gains a different point of view. He understands the play, recognizes other possibilities of reacting and influencing the course of the play, sees what is necessary in his situation and what reaction is the most promising at the current moment. And he also recognizes from the perspective of the auditorium how the piece will develop if he reacts in another way. He is no longer caught in the old self-image. And he succeeds at being amused about the "play on the stage."

Back on the stage he slips completely into his role again, experiencing and living out the piece with all of its aspects. He enjoys the play and can even totally dedicate himself to the dramatic parts of the piece. But he is no longer caught in his role or unconscious of it. He knows that there is another reality and that he himself can influence the progress of the play.

A friend's experience during the time in which she worked with *Maha Chohan* illustrates its effect: A women told her that she has cancer and is in an intense emotional crisis as a result.

My friend thought about what it would probably be like if she herself developed cancer and pictured herself in this state. She normally avoided imagining illness and death because these were connected with a great deal of fear for her. However, at this moment it was very easy for her and she had the feeling: "Right now you consider your entire life to be an experiment, so it's interesting to also look at this situation and experience it in your mind."

A similar situation followed a few days later: She wanted to drive to a seminar and had a stretch of about 60 kilometers ahead of her. It was January, the streets were icy, and it began to snow. She was in a panic about the slippery streets and worried about losing control over her car. She had had a very unpleasant experience years before that she still dwelled on and it caused her to avoid using the car when it snowed, if possible. So she was quite disturbed after driving for 15 minutes and decided to turn around. However, a completely new thought occurred to her: "If you turn around now, you'll just sit at home and be aggravated. Just simply look at what happens if you continue to drive. In any case, it's more exciting than sitting at home." She made it to the seminar in good shape.

The essence of *Maha Chohan* also helps people who are very sensitive and take in more from the surrounding world than they can process, who have a hard time drawing the line. Such people easily sense the mood that's "in the air," the emotional states that other people are in, and may even also perceive subtle beings. If they do not set limits, they lose themselves.

This energy supports counselors, therapists, teachers, and managers in accompanying people without being caught up in the problems and opinions of others. From the distance they can more easily perceive causes, backgrounds, and new possibilities. They can help the other person use his own wisdom and don't always have to find the solution for the client themselves. They gain the ability of giving the other person what he really needs and thereby express themselves in a way that the other person understands. Their interactions with others are distinguished by clarity, respect, and love.

Another difficult factor in working with people is that the therapist (coach, etc.) encounters his own weak points as well. With the essence it becomes easier to maintain a distance or deal with one's own blind spot.

Through the necessary distance to the outer world, the energy also helps a person find his own center. The connection to inner wisdom and the Higher Self opens up here. We perceive that it's totally natural to be connected with the cosmic consciousness. This is a part of our existence.

The Meditation

Imagine that you are in the Himalayas, at a spot from which you can look out into the world. There is a pleasantly cool temperature at this place. You are surrounded by a light-blue sky, snow-covered mountains, and the stony mountain is beneath your feet.

First look at the earth from here and then at your own life.

In moments in which you are very entangled and caught up in your life, simply enjoy being at this place of expansiveness, coolness, and sublimity. Repeat the word "sublimity" often in your thoughts, and let this feeling arise within you, let it pulsate throughout your entire body—"sublimity."

The Message

I greet you, my friends, from my place in the Himalayas. This is the center of my spiritual strength. It is connected with the earth, with the depths of the earth, and yet still high up in the heavens. Here the earth is present in its massive form of rock and yet expansiveness and clarity reign. Here the water element that represents feelings is snow.

I greet you and I teach you to live the divinity in this world, to be connected with this earth and at the same time be sublime, uplifted above the entanglements. On this earth that I love so much, on this earth you can learn to merge the expression of divinity with your earthly life and to let the blossom of divinity arise from the ground of the earth and unfold. And this is a task and an opportunity that is only possible on the earth, a place where a tremendous variety of emotions and experiences are possible. A great spectrum is possible here on the earth, and I teach you to be at a distance and at the same time in the middle of events. I teach you to be both the actor on the stage, to sit in the auditorium, and to direct the play.

Yet, it is first important to perceive that you are entangled in the play with your heart and soul, that you are wrapped up in it, and that you watch it at the same time. If you watch it and are uninvolved, you are missing out on a learning experience.

Be in the middle of life, be lively and let yourselves be intoxicated by the waves of life, by the joy and liveliness of life, by the heights and depths of life. Be drunken with life and simultaneously sense your sublimity, your divinity, the divine core.

No. 2—*Lao Tse*

Acceptance and Inner Peace

The Effect of the Master Essence

This essence helps a person to stop judging and condemning. It lets us perceive that every situation, every human being, and every occurrence has many aspects. There are advantages *and* disadvantages in everything.

It allows us to accept facts and act and decide in accordance with them instead of getting excited about things that have happened and complaining about the past.

It leads us to stop and take the necessary pause before acting by collecting the strength for the next step.

It helps us achieve a deeper level of meditation, as well as inner calm and composure.

Associated with the chakras: Sacral chakra (throat chakra)
Color: Blue (royal blue)
Tarot card: No. 10—The Wheel of Fortune (Fortune)
Gemstone: Sapphire
Oil application: Lower stomach area and sacral vertebra, as well as larynx and throat

A person who has balanced this aspect:

- Can observe situations, see other people, and perceive events without judging them.
- Can accept himself as he is; recognizes that he's neither good nor bad.
- Recognizes what is valuable about every form of being and every situation.
- Doesn't restrict his viewpoint and also sees aspects that are unpleasant for him; perceives everything.
- Can see and accept the changes that occur in life.
- Accepts every event with inner peace; reacts calmly.
- Looks to see what is right at precisely this moment and knows that everything may be completely different in the next mo-

ment; makes decisions in the present moment; takes an exact look at things and recognizes all the necessary facts.
- Has the right rhythm for phases of work and rest; gathers his strength before taking the next step.

A person who has not yet balanced this aspect:
- Strongly condemns others; thinks in terms of black-and-white; everything is divided into "good" and "bad" and filed into categories; takes action according to the principle of "either-or"; as a result, overlooks many things and comes up with unrealistic appraisals.
- Condemns himself; quickly feels himself to be condemned and rejected by others.
- Blocks himself because of his judgments (I don't do this because it's bad).
- Has self-doubts; believes he's worthless or less valuable than others.
- Has a tendency to be a perfectionist, nothing is good enough.
- Can't create any new perspectives because he's too caught up in his beliefs (that won't work because...; I can't do this; if I do this, then this and that will happen).
- Takes action on the basis of an inner state of hectic; condemns inner peace as lack of drive, apathy, and laziness.
- Suffers from stress as a result of supposed chains of cause and effect (I must do this because otherwise...).
- Forces others to become hectic because of his own state of being hectic; is always "charged up."
- Lives more in the future or the past than in the present.
- Gets involved in strong emotional reactions because he defends himself against the facts and doesn't want to accept them.

But also a person who:
- Is lethargic or has fallen into an inner rigidity; is so calm that it paralyzes him; to whom nothing matters.
- Overrates his own value.

Description

While *Maha Chohan* lets us take a step back, *Lao Tse* leads us to the infinity of the current moment, into the here and now. *Maha Chohan* prepares us and *Lao Tse* is the implementation—life in the here and now.

Being in the present moment makes it possible for us to experience calmness, expansiveness, and composure. This state may be unusual at the start since we often judge inner peace to be a lack of drive, apathy, or laziness. It appears that taking action isn't possible in this state, as if there were no energy available with which to act. Many people associate the condition of calmness with meditation or vacation.

Working in a state of inner peace also makes it possible to experience a new quality of work. We no longer have a hectic work style, but act consistently and calmly from our own center. The correct proportions and the right time for tension and relaxation, for action and rest are then found. Some people may have to become accustomed to this at first.

If we become hectic or stressed, the energy of *Lao Tse* supports us in coming back to our own center and finding calmness and composure. Our own composed emanation then influences the other people in our environment as well and lets them become calmer.

When we consciously live the present moment, each situation is new. We are no longer caught up in the patterns and beliefs of the past or the images that we've already created for the future. It therefore becomes possible to react in a new way, to include all the facts of a situation in the here and now, and to take action in a different way—instead of once again mechanically playing out old patterns of behavior. When we are in the current moment, other people can no longer influence us as easily since the buttons for the familiar patterns of behavior no longer function.

And we stop condemning, dividing things into good and bad, and filing them into categories. We recognize the polarity, the differences, how things oscillate between the extremes, and we accept it. This means that we no longer get struck in one extreme and no longer hang onto what appears to be good. Instead, we remain in motion. We accept our life in the duality.

Once we are free of judgments that come from the past, we can perceive situations realistically and in their totality. We develop a sense of reality and observe other people with a more differentiated perspective.

Those who work with the essence of *Lao Tse* will also be confronted with the issue of self-worth. Here the judgments and appraisals of one's own self again come into focus and the questions about what a person can and can't do once again become visible. We ask ourselves if we are better or worse than other people. We see through our game of "putting someone on a pedestal" in order to throw him back down again and putting ourselves up there instead. Then it's possible to see through the game of above and below, of being better or worse, and accept others as they are. It's possible to see the worth of every person and every being.

Those who can observe without judging perceive the constant state of change in life. Opposites follow each other—love follows hate, days of sadness are followed by days of joy, bad luck follows good luck, a high point follows every low point, and rain follows the sunshine. One day we wake up in the morning full of drive, and the next day we're tired and in a bad mood. Yet, when we are at our center, we are the observer who remains untouched by these changes. We know that the only consistent thing is change and that those who find themselves in these fluctuations on the outside get thrown back and forth. On the periphery of the cyclone we may get dizzy, but there is calm at the center. The ups and downs of life can be looked at, accepted, and put to use with composure from the perspective of this center.

A woman suffered very much after the death of her dog, which had eaten poison. A few hours after the application of the essence, she was able to accept its death and let go of the pain.

When we no longer *identify* with the events around us, our fears fall away. When we see fear for what it is, namely a feeling like any other, it has little influence on us. However, if we identify with it, if we are in the middle of fear, this creates a series of further thoughts and feelings that intensify this state. We seek the causes for this fear and this creates a cause-and-effect chain that possibly doesn't even exist. Events are no longer seen from a neutral standpoint but are considered to be confirmations.

Everything appears to confirm this fear—events and occurrences are observed and interpreted from this perspective.

One example: It's a bright day. You are sitting in a room and hear a sound. In most cases, you wouldn't even register this sound consciously or would immediately forget it again.

The difference today is that you watched a horror film last night. You virtually listen for any sound and, when you hear one, become startled.

At such moments, the energy of *Lao Tse* makes it possible to perceive that identification with the inner state, as in this situation, is colored by the fear of perception. The same can be said for other perceptions and feelings.

> *As long as we identify ourselves with something,*
> *we live in shackles.*
> WEI WU WEI

When we stop judging and identifying with things, the events of life can then be accepted as opportunities for learning, as challenges that allow us to grow. Whether the situations are pleasant or unpleasant is no longer so important since both are learning steps and both are equally valid.

One example may illustrate this point: When we build a house and have ordered white windows of synthetic material, but wooden windows are delivered, we have the opportunity of sending back the wooden windows or installing them. We don't have to be annoyed since the delivery is a fact that requires us to make a decision. Although the decision has varying aftereffects since the house will look different and synthetic windows will create another set of problems than wooden windows, no matter whether we accept the delivery or not, further events will occur. We always learn, no matter what we decide.

Everything is a learning step and an experience—there are no right ones and no wrong ones. However, for us human beings there is a more pleasant way and a less agreeable way, a way that feels good and a way that creates difficulties. These are experiences as well.

This energy helps us to take the path, accept whatever we encounter along the way, and feel free to act.

"I've been working with Lao Tse and acceptance for two weeks now. I've had enough of waiting and twiddling my thumbs. Now I finally want to do something again," was the reaction of a woman seminar participant as she once again drew *Lao Tse.* This reaction shows what "acceptance" means for many people, namely: put up with things since you can't change them; don't get excited but swallow your reactions. To them, it means not taking action.

However, this isn't its meaning. Acceptance means seeing the facts without sticking them into the category of "good or bad," without becoming annoyed or getting into a quarrel. What happens is neither depressing nor exciting. It's simply the facts of life. Our judgment gives things the coloration of good or bad. And what appears bad to me may be good for others: "Damn it, it's raining," complains the person who's giving a garden party. "What luck, now I don't need to water," says the owner of a garden in delight.

Just as the energy helps us to let go of our constant judging, it also helps us overcome lethargy and apathy. Being non-judgmental doesn't mean being fatalistic or helplessly letting everything happen.

Some people become panicked and believe that they immediately have to change everything when they have attained a bit of self-knowledge. However, when they accept that things are like they are at the moment, they can calmly make decisions about changes and find the best point in time for these changes. And some patterns of behavior can be left alone for the time being because other things are more important at the moment or they aren't quite ready for a change yet. Then there is nothing more about it that's good or bad.

Acceptance is also the precondition for trust, love, and self-love. Some people won't be able to work with the energy of *Christ* or *Lady Nada* if they haven't learned in advance to assent to and lovingly accept perceptions and reactions.

That acceptance must precede love becomes clear when we fall in love. Then we are totally in the current moment—an encounter takes place in the here and now. Looking into each other's eyes leads to a lucid moment.

Acceptance is also the precondition for transformation. Only an individual who has accepted his undesirable ways of behaving as an indication of his own shadow aspects and unpleasant experiences as necessary perceptions can make use of these experiences in order to become healed and learn what he lacks.

Lao Tse brings us into the present moment, and this is meditation. This energy brings us into a "no-mind" state, into the innermost core that remains untouched by the constant ups and downs of life. Consciousness and self-knowledge is possible there. The connection to existence opens us up since existence is always in the current moment. It is outside of time and space, and we come into contact with it because we are also in the present moment.

The Meditation

Imagine that you are sitting with your back leaned against the trunk of a tree. Feel the energy that flows into the leaves from the roots, and hear the soft rustling of the leaves in the wind. You look out onto a wide, expansive clear land, a grassland in which there are no other trees or just a single tree here and there. On the horizon you see mountains that enclose this expanse.

Sit there and simply look at this grassland, the expanse, the clarity, with the blue sky above you.

As your next step, get a sense of the tree. It is a tall tree.

Then become this tree. Stretch your roots down into the earth. Feel how the trunk is strong and tall, and then stretch your leaves up into the sky. Now stand there as this tree, old and with deep roots, and look out across the wide land as this tree. Feel what the tree feels, see what the tree sees, and hear what the tree hears.

When you are ready to go even further, start the third part of the meditation. At the place where you have been sitting at this tree, I, *Lao Tse*, now sit and look across the wide land. And you, as the tree, hear my words. You hear the message that I bring to the world and to you. It is the message for this moment, and it will be short and clear.

In closing, once again become yourself as you sit against the tree and come out of this meditation.

The Message

I greet you and surround you with the energy of clarity, expansiveness, and farsightedness.

I, *Lao Tse*, support you human beings in finding your truth and clarity—in recognizing it, seeing through it, and accepting it since only what you accept can be transformed. When people want to transform something in order to get rid of it, this has only a limited effect. True change can only occur by accepting something, lovingly taking it to heart the way it is, and keeping your eyes open for the goal and the path with which you want to reach it. Accept what exists at the present moment.

Do this in the same way you would if you had a child who has just turned four and begins to read the first letters of the alphabet. At this moment you accept your child just like it is. You accept that it is just beginning to read. You accept that it makes mistakes because it is just starting off on its path. The child has its eyes on a goal: learning to read. If you would scold it for each mistake, if you would be dissatisfied, or if you would want to get rid of the mistakes that it makes as quickly as possible, then you would put pressure on the child and it would learn more slowly and make more mistakes because it would be afraid. And it will not reach this goal in joy. Rejoice with it over the steps that it is taking, over its liveliness. Accept the child as it is, with the mistakes that it makes in learning, and support it in its learning steps. Then it will enjoy reading and very quickly achieve its goal.

Treat yourselves in the same way as well: accept things as they are. Look at yourselves, get to the bottom of things, ask questions and more questions, go deeper and deeper until you have reached the roots, until you find the roots, until you discover that everything has the same origins. And when you have reached this point, then you can go beyond everything into a new dimension.

I support you in seeing clearly, in accepting, in being calm and loving with yourselves, in seeing this world as an observer, and using life as a mirror for your development. I teach you to observe, to assent to things, to accept, and to transform yourselves as a result. This is because with every layer that you accept, you go one step farther down to the root in order to then go beyond it.

No. 3—El Morya

Trust

The Effect of the Master Essence

This essence strengthens a person's basic trust, the trust in oneself, in other people, and in existence. As a result, fears are diminished.

It supports a realistic evaluation of one's own abilities and those of other people.

It supports therapeutic work on the prenatal and early childhood period with respect to traumas and shocks to basic trust (for example: rebirthing, prenatal massage, and primal therapy).

Associated with the chakras: Solar plexus chakra (base and crown chakra)
Color: Aquamarine
Tarot card: No. 1—The Magician
Gemstone: Blue aquamarine, blue topaz, lapis lazuli
Oil application: Lower stomach area, below the collarbone (zones of fear), as well as knees, around the navel, around the larynx

A person who has balanced this aspect:

- Has basic trust.
- Has trust in his own abilities; trusts that he will be successful, that he will receive support, that the right thing will happen, that he has the ability to solve every occurring problem within himself.
- Has self-confidence and starts to take action, even if he isn't perfect yet; knows that mistakes are learning steps and doesn't let himself be intimidated by them.
- Realistically evaluates his own abilities; has the courage to act; has the courage to apply and try out the knowledge and abilities he has acquired.

- Has trust in the support from the subtle world (God, the masters, the angels, the earth).
- Trusts other people; can get involved in relationships.
- Entrusts other people with tasks; recognizes what they are capable of and what's too much for them.

A person who has not yet balanced this aspect:
- Doesn't have trust in his own abilities; has little self-confidence ("I can't do that, I'm not capable enough for that, I'm not good enough") and is therefore insecure in his behavior and his abilities.
- Doesn't have trust in existence; believes that "no one will help me, I have to do everything alone."
- Has inhibitions making contact with other people; is very shy, insecure, and reserved.
- Has a strong mistrust of other people; ends up isolated as a result.
- Isn't capable of having relationships because he can't trust and open up to another person.
- Suffers from intense fears: fears related to existence, fear of not surviving, fear of failure, fear of the unknown (because the basic trust has been lost).
- Suffers from a strong fear of loss, resulting in jealousy.
- Is afraid of everything that can't been seen but sensed or felt (such as subtle manifestations).
- Suffers from tensions because of fear (drawn-up shoulders).

But also a person who:
- Has an exaggerated sense of self-assurance: thinks he's capable of everything and doesn't recognize his own limitations.
- Displays excessive trust in others, is constantly deceived and yet continues to trust; believes everything that others say and has unlimited trust in others.
- Has exaggerated trust in help from the outside: "I don't need to do anything, existence is sure to do it for me, I only have to trust."

The difference between No. 3—El Morya and
No. 6—Djwal Khul on the theme of "self-confidence"

No. 3   strengthens self-confidence by abolishing fears.
No. 6   strengthens by boosting knowledge about one's own
        strength.

The difference between No. 3—El Morya and
No. 2—Lao Tse on the theme of "fear"

No. 3 helps by overcoming the fears through trust.
No. 2 helps overcome fears through acceptance and the reduc-
        tion of identification.

Description

The energy of *El Morya* teaches us trust in ourselves, in our own
strength (3rd chakra), in the earth (1st chakra), and in the support of the whole (7th chakra). This essence brings us back into
contact with basic trust, the connection to existence that we once
had while we were safe and secure in the womb. As a result, it
also heals the oppressive traumas and shocks of the prenatal
period and early childhood. It transforms the unpleasant experiences of being deserted, helplessly at the mercy of others, and
separated—all of which lead to mistrust and fear. The essence
therefore also supports the work of primal therapy, rebirthing, or
other forms of therapy that work on such traumas.

Trust is like a solid ground on which we can stand and walk.

The greater the mistrust and the fear, the most strength and
courage will leave us. Fears causes us to be reserved, not try
out our strengths and abilities, and be satisfied with less than is
actually possible. It leads us to lazy compromises that we regret
and yet still don't end.

The fear of mistakes, blame, and failure is probably deeply
rooted in all human beings. Behind all of this is ultimately the
fear of being rejected.

Trust dissolves what has previously hindered us in seeing and
using our own abilities. As result of self-confidence, there is an
increase in the courage to put the abilities and acquired knowledge to use and go into the "outside world" with one's own abil-

ities. The sentence: "I'm not good enough yet, I can't do it yet" can only be overcome by taking action, trying things out, and practicing. "Practice makes perfect" is the common saying. It's normal for mistakes to happen while practicing since mistakes are learning experiences that show us how things don't work. However, mistakes are not failure. Only those who have the self-assurance to go to the limits and risk failure can overcome limitations and grow.

Trust is the foundation of every new step. Going into something new means changing oneself and encountering a new type of behavior, a new environment, and/or new people. When an individual risks this step, he will leave old qualities behind him.

As we stood at the Frankfurt Book Fair with this book and the essences, a woman came by who listened to the conversations in a rather unconcentrated manner. When she drew a card with the question: "Which essence will support me the most at the moment," the theme of "trust" came up (No. 3—*El Morya*). As she rubbed some oil on her pulse, she immediately noticed that she became more calm, powerful, and self-confident. Very delighted about this, she told me that she had written a book and was actually supposed to have an appointment with a publisher half-an-hour earlier. However, the appointment had been postponed and she had wandered around in a nervous and agitated way. While doing so, she had "coincidentally" come across the essences.

She came back the next day to tell me that her meeting had been a success and that she had felt very calm and centered during the entire conversation.

Another woman who used the essence reported about its effect upon her son. He had started school a short time before and suffered from a "nervous bladder." This means that he had to go to the toilet every half-hour and disrupted the class as a result. The woman then rubbed his belly with the oil No. 3—*El Morya*, which he very much enjoyed and also reminded her of if she forgot it. After a few days, his condition had improved. Now he only had to use the toilet during the breaks, which means every full hour.

Trust is the foundation for every relationship. The development of self-confidence allows us to become more self-secure and enables us to appear self-assured. The result is an inner calm, an open and natural way of expressing oneself, and more ease in making contact with other people. The essence is therefore suitable for people who have difficulties in making contact because they are afraid of others or mistrustful.

One woman who used the essences reported that she met very interesting people after having used the *El Morya* essence. It occurred to her that she had previously avoided these people because a lack of self-confidence.

We can also open up more in intimate relationships when we have greater trust. Trust is the precondition for devotion and love.

Another women who used the essences found the courage to talk to her partner in life about problems and bothersome habits that she had previously kept silent about. As a result, both of them were able to make a fresh start in the relationship.

The energy of *El Morya* also strengthens trust in the feminine and masculine principles. The essence supports us in confronting themes related to the father and the mother, healing wounds. Applying the essence around the navel strengthens trust in a person's own feminine power and the trust in a person's own masculine power is boosted when it's applied around the larynx. Both areas are significant for men and women since every individual contains both aspects.

Trust in the source, in God, strengthens the connection and opens up the permeability for impulses from the Higher Self. As a result, one's own intuition can be better perceived and put to use.

As we started to work with *El Morya*, we were once again plagued by the paralyzing fears that we had known in the past. There were suddenly unfounded economic fears, fear of the future, and the fear of going hungry and having to sleep under bridges. We went through all of this once again and then achieved trust in ourselves and in existence. Since that time, these strong fears haven't come up again.

This experience shows that trust and fear are closely connected with each other. We often still remember fearful experiences from childhood days that no longer have any basis today.

Fear strongly colors our perceptions. A person is constantly on guard, "sees danger behind every bush," reacts in a tense and inappropriate way and therefore also creates irritability and defensiveness in the surrounding world. The constant tension makes a person tired and lets important things be overseen. And it ultimately leads to tensions in the body that can often be recognized by a person having drawn-up shoulders.

Fear also restricts the ability to think and an individual's creativity.

Fear blocks the flow of energy and makes the aura shrink— love and trust stretch the aura. If we are in love and trust, we can detach ourselves from our fears and trustingly open up to something new (also see No. 2—*Lao Tse* on the theme of fear).

The Meditation

Imagine that you are standing in front of an archway, a light-blue archway. There are no doors in it but just a light-blue archway. Behind it there is an entire series of these light-blue archways, just like we sometimes see rows of rose espaliers.

Read the inscription on the archway. It may be that the first inscription says "trust in yourself," "trust in the earth," or "trust in higher forms of energy."

Then walk through the first archway of trust very self-confidently and perceive what happens within you. At the moment in which you walk through it, you gain this quality. You gain it within yourself and it fills you from the feet to the tips of your hair. It fills all the layers of your aura.

Then end the meditation for today and let the newly won energy have its effect within you and expand itself.

The following day, go into a meditation at the place where you ended your meditation the day before. Look again at the archway that is in front of you and also look at the one or ones that are behind you.

Then read the inscription of the archway in front of you and walk through it.

You will become increasingly trusting and open up more and more to this process. Also look at what is resisting within you. If there is an archway that you don't want to go through yet, then wait and remain standing in front of it. Look at your resistance. You can place what you want to cast aside at the foot of the archway and leave it there.

Take your time. Only when you are willing—and this may take days—should you walk through the archway.

The Message

I greet you and send you the energy of trust, trust in your own power and strength, in how you guide yourselves, in the aspects that you call the "Higher Self," the trust in the higher levels of consciousness that in turn are ultimately just aspects of the divine, all-encompassing being, of your own self. We, the masters of the master level, are also energies that are reflected within you. You bear all of these energies and aspects within yourselves as well, and this is why we can be effective and support you.

Everything is connected with everything else. Everything vibrates in divine love. What are you afraid of if everything is in the love and you yourselves are in the love? There are light and shadow aspects on the earth. But all of this is a mirror of your own existence. And as long as you still find the shadow aspects to be threatening, there will be aspects within yourselves that you ignore and don't accept. If you succeed in achieving trust once again, trust in the divine love. Then there will no longer be fear. Then you will be free of fear. What should you be afraid of if you are enveloped in love, if you are connected with everything and are one with everything?

Trust means finding your way back to your own divine core and the state of oneness, perceiving that everything that happens is all right—that everything that happens is a step on your path and that you always have support, even in the darkest places in your lives. They belong to it as well. They are learning experiences that you have created yourself, in which you are given support. You have enough strength and energy to get through them and take the learning steps. For every problem that you have created, you have also taken the solution with you.

You cannot train yourself to be trusting. You can most quickly achieve it by once again connecting yourselves with your own divinity.

No. 4—*Kwan Yin*

Dedication

The Effect of the Master Essence

This essence helps us to flow with what's happening and to really become involved with things. It therefore supports people who hesitate in opening up to something new and unfamiliar, as well as ultimately life itself.

It gets congested, rigid feelings flowing so that they can heal.

It opens up the access to our own feelings, helps us express them and live them out.

It is very helpful in doing mourning work and for people who hold back their tears and can't cry.

It can get bodily fluids flowing (for example, a stuffy nose).

Associated with the chakras: Heart chakra (crown chakra)
Color: Coral
Tarot card: No. 9—The Hermit
Gemstone: Rainbow moonstone, watermelon tourmaline, green
   garnet
Oil application: Chest area and 7th cervical vertebra, as well as
   for the increase of lymphatic flow on the points for the lym-
   phatic flow (see illustration on page 96).

A person who has balanced this aspect:
- Is curious about life and is adventuresome; jumps into life and lets himself be surprised; joyfully says "yes" to life.
- Uses his own strengths, power, and abilities in the flow of life.
- Knows when he must act and when he should let things happen (intuition).
- Takes action with all his strength when the time to act has come.
- Has access to his feelings and can show them; spontaneously expresses feelings; shows how he feels at the moment.
- Is in the flow; can accept changes; knows that "the only constant thing is change."

- Swims through the highs and lows of life; doesn't get stuck in them.
- Lets himself fall into feelings without sinking in them.
- Has empathy and tolerance.

A person who has not yet balanced this aspect:
- Has no access to his feels, holds them back and cuts himself off from them.
- Is afraid of letting himself go.
- Inwardly sits on a powder keg of undigested feelings like anger, sadness, and fear.
- Can't express feelings; tears are held back and not cried; has a stone on his heart.
- Has extremely strong self-control; others usually can't tell what's going on inside of him.
- Moves in a stiff way.
- Suffers from strong inner tensions and cramps; the nerves are tensed to the breaking point because feelings are suppressed and he's afraid of letting go inside, afraid of what would happen and the things at which he needs to take a second.
- Holds onto the old for fear of change; has difficulty in directing his vision to the future.
- Is afraid of adventure, of change, of what will come tomorrow, of what life brings with it; doesn't get involved in things that are new and unfamiliar or only does so with great hesitation.
- Is afraid of the day as it begins in the morning.
- Often uses the word "must."
- Only feels good when he can plan and control events.

But also a person who:
- Lets life flow away without acting at the right moment; is lethargic.

The difference between No. 4—Kwan Yin and No. 17—Pallas Athene on the theme of "expressing feelings":

No. 4   dissolves old, congested, and blocked feelings and opens access to the emotions.

No. 17   helps to spontaneously and naturally express the momentary feelings.

The difference between No. 4—Kwan Yin and No. 10—Kamakura on the theme of "taking action":

No. 4   tends to strengthen the passive side of taking action, letting things happen, and acting in harmony with the flow of life. It helps release control and the act of holding on. We release fears and they heal as a result.

No. 10   brings the energy for the deed and strengthens actively taking action at the right point in time. The transformation of fears happens through positive experiences.

Description

Those who trust can easily go into the flow of life. Those who dedicate themselves are as curious about life as a child who is astonished at the world and its happenings, who is open to its occurrences. Children are open when they feel secure. Their intuition often warns them about dangerous situations.

Dedication doesn't mean fatalistically devoting oneself to everything, doing nothing, or disregarding one's own perception and intuition. True dedication includes one's own strength and power. It uses one's own abilities in order to swim with the flow of life and be in harmony with the life plan. This requires less effort.

Those who have the courage to get involved can experience that they are carried along and receive support.

The image of a duck on a stream illustrates what is meant here. The duck has enough strength to swim against the current or get out of the stream. However, it lets itself be carried by the water, additionally uses its own strength and paddles with its feet in order to move forwards more quickly. It uses the current in order to progress without effort, without resistance, and enjoys the rapids and whirlpools.

This doesn't mean "swimming with the tide." One individual's own flow in life can be completely different from that of another person. It may contain paths and actions that others don't understand. Sometimes there are very few people who can understand us and accept us when we take our own paths. Dedication to oneself is self-realization. And there may be sections of this path where we are completely alone.

The opposite pole to dedication is control. Some people try to maintain control by excessively thinking things through and structuring their planning and organization very precisely. However, as a result they block their own intuition and "lucky coincidences," missing out on the unexpected gifts of existence. *Kwan Yin* helps us let go of the need to be in control.

The energy of *Kwan Yin* supports us in more quickly perceiving whether we are acting in harmony with our life plan. We more quickly recognize whether the difficulties serve to "train our strength" or whether they are indications that this path doesn't get us any further. It lets us perceive our own strength, responsibility, and our path in life. Those who just allow themselves to be carried along by events are responsible for them as well.

When a person lives in harmony, he will know when to take action and apply his own power—and when he should just let things happen. This is the fulfillment of the prayer: "Give me the strength to act when I should act. Give me the patience to wait when I should wait. And give me the wisdom to know when I should act and when I should wait."

One theme of the *Kwan-Yin* energy is structure and chaos. As in "taking action and letting things happen," it brings these two poles into balance. Rigid, constrictive structures are dissolved and chaotic energies are purposefully guided into a proper channel and become effective as a result. This helps people who have a rigid, constrictive view of the world, who feel themselves forced to do things and not free because of this. These people frequently use the word "must" and have an allergic react to compulsions from the outside when someone else says to them: "you must...".

The essence promotes the courage to get involved in some-thing new and have new experiences.

This essence also supports people who live without any plans and in chaos and want to bring more structure and purpose into their lives—or those who oscillate between structuring every-thing down to the last detail and chaos. Such people spend hours cleaning their desk and living space, making sure every-thing is perfect down to the last detail. Then they do nothing more and a new chaos is created.

This Master Essence helps direct a person's energy and guide it into channels. They support an individual in assuming re-sponsibility for his actions and goals and in making the decision as to which plans to follow up on. This is the preparation for the *Christ* energy.

"Everything that flows is healthy," says the well-known heal-ing practitioner Peter Mandel. And the energy of *Kwan Yin* starts whatever is congested or held back flowing. Its effect is compa-rable to that of water as it flows against an obstacle until it wash-es or clears it away.

The same also applies to rigid, fixed structures in which some-one is caught, as well as for emotions that are held back. Tears that haven't been cried begin to flow, suppressed traumas are washed away, and feelings start to move again.

One woman who uses the essences suffered from asthma and often had difficulty getting enough air at night. Just as she started using the *Kwan Yin* Essence, she woke up for about ten nights in a row at 2 a.m. and "wept barrels." Afterwards, she felt lighter, got enough air, and could peacefully go back to sleep. After these ten days, her lungs had become more free and much mucous had flowed out.

Another woman user was suffering the pangs of love and took a bath, into which she put the *Kwan Yin* oil. She became con-scious of her suppressed desires and disappointments and cried for three hours. Afterwards, she felt better.

The essence gets the energy of a blocked emotional body flowing again. The mental blocks of feelings like "I'm not al-lowed to cry, I'm not allowed to show my feelings, I have no access to my feeling," are also undermined since the energy works directly in the emotional body and in the heart chakra.

Men in particular are sometimes surprised that feeling of sadness and tears come with this essence.

Kwan Yin opens the energy of the heart in a gentle and loving way. Its energy heals the heart chakra and the astral body of wounds, lets "the stone fall from the heart," and frees us inside. During the cleansing phase it may be that oppressive feelings are perceived very intensely and a person feels blue as a result. However, we won't sink into the emotions or be flooded by them. We maintain an observer's position that lovingly participates in the processes and ultimately leads us to an inner peace and relaxation or to a cheerful state of repose.

A friend told me that her husband makes an impression of cheerfulness and relaxation all day long when he takes the *Kwan Yin* essence.

Not only are we more tolerant and loving towards ourselves, but we also develop more compassion and understanding for the people around us—without suffering along with them. This compassion arises from the loving connection with all other beings. When we don't experience ourselves as separate but feel connected, our well-being is associated with that of other people. This is like a mother who is happy when her child is doing well.

The *Kwan Yin* essence can also dissolve tensions on the physical level that arise because of emotional or mental clinging. When applied to the lymphatic points (see illustration on page 96), it supports the self-healing powers of the body in cases of colds, headaches, and sinusitis. A stuffy nose may start to run as a result.

The Meditation

Look at how a duck swims down a stream. The duck, itself a powerful animal, lets itself be carried by the stream as it flows along—sometimes slowly, sometimes quickly, sometimes in swirls. And it follows the flow. Only when there are obstacles in the way does it swim past them. It can use its own strength at any time. Sometimes it even paddles with its feet in order to swim more quickly than the river. Yet, it doesn't hang onto the sides and get stuck in the trees. It either swims lightly within this

flow and lets itself be carried and is carried, or it ends this flowing and goes its own way.

We also have the power to do what we want in this way. We
are not like leaves that are at the mercy of this flowing without a
will. Instead, we have our own will. Yet, we can use this will to be
in the flow and observe what happens in the stream.

Become the duck that lets itself be carried by the flow. Take
an exact look at the stream: is it a mountain torrent or does it
flow calmly? Is the bed of the stream sandy or does it have
stones in it? Are the stones pointed or round? Does the stream
have many bends and curves or is it does it have a straight course?
Are you in danger of being driven up on the shore or can you
swim in the middle of it? Are you surrounded by other ducks
that swim together with you or are you alone? What is your
feeling as you are carried by the water? Are you fearful or do
you also enjoy the ride when it's fast? Do you trust your own
power and the feeling of being carried along? Do you trust nature? Look at your surroundings, perceive your feelings, and
dedicate yourself to life.

Become conscious of the fears that you have, and let the
fears that you want to let go of become a leaf that departs from
you and is carried away by the flow of life.

The Message

I greet you and teach you dedication, the dedication to life and
the things that happen—to be filled with love as you live your
lives and filled with love as you do the things you do. I teach you
to perceive the beauty in everything that you do, no matter whether it is garden work, looking at a rose, or working at the PC. You
can be in everything with love and dedication by opening yourselves and connecting yourselves with everything that is. You
can let yourselves flow and be in the flow. You can let yourselves
be carried without denying your own strength and power.

Dedicating oneself to life is like bathing in the ocean, is like
being carried along, is like swimming in a quiet lake. It is like
swimming in a river. It is like a leaf blown away by the wind.
Sometimes things are still and sometimes they are very lively.
There is sadness and joy. Sometimes it is time to live out one's

power and put it to use, and then it is time to receive and to harvest. This is how life changes. And those who can dedicate themselves will be carried along on their own. They will be carried along by the cosmos.

All those who are filled with sadness, who are full of troubles and worries, full of suffering and pain—all these will be comforted and healed by my energy. They will be freed from the old and whatever burdens them so intensely, if they are willing to let go of the heavy things and dedicate themselves to being.

Then I will envelope you with my love so that you can once again live joyfully. So that the heaviness falls away from you and you are once again lively in the current moment.

No. 5—*Christ*

Truth and Unconditional Love

The Effect of the Master Essence

This essence connects with the heart energy and brings a person into contact with truth, unconditional love, and the love of fellow beings.

It supports us in examining our own beliefs and the values of society time and again.

When the essence is applied to the hand chakras, it opens the energy flow of the *Christ* vibration. It is therefore helpful for body workers and people who work with the sick.

It supports work on problems related to the father and the theme of "authority."

It supports the process of finding oneself, also during puberty.

Associated with the chakras: Throat chakra (heart chakra)
Color: Red (ruby red)
Tarot card: No. 4—The Emperor
Gemstone: Ruby, yellow diamond
Oil application: Front of throat, nape of neck, beneath the collarbone (zone of fear, see illustration on page 96), between the shoulder blades; in addition, on the hand chakras (inside of palms)

A person who has balanced this aspect:
• Knows his own truth, values, wishes and needs, and lives accordingly.
• Takes responsibility for his actions.
• Checks time and again to see if his own actions correspond with his own truth and changes his actions, if necessary.
• Can accept and respect other people's outlooks and truth; doesn't have to convince others of his own opinion.
• Can accept and reflect on criticism and contradictions, but doesn't let himself be limited by these opinions—lives his own truth instead.

- Is loving towards all being, towards people, plants, animals—this love is related to concrete things and not just abstract; acts in love for the good of the earth, for all being, for all people.
- Recognizes that love is connected with accepting the other and that providing for the other's highest good and acting out of love for others can be painful (for example, not giving alcohol to an alcoholic going through withdrawal, even if he begs for it).
- Has enough farsightedness to perceive what is truly best for others.
- Has leadership qualities; leads on the basis of strength and love, for the benefit of others and for the good of the whole (as Frederick the Great said: "The ruler is the first servant of his state").
- Can bring the good of the whole into harmony with the good of the individual.
- Lives his natural authority without ruler airs.
- Doesn't avoid conflicts with others, but also doesn't provoke them; is clear in confrontations, shows understanding for the other person, is open for the other person's opinion, and examines his own opinion.
- Has connected his willpower with love.

A person who has not yet balanced this aspect:
- Has strong self-doubts.
- Doesn't live according to his own truth.
- Feels himself to be small, incapable, and a failure; hides behind others; is afraid of punishment like a small child fears an authoritarian father.
- Has problems with authorities; voluntarily subordinates himself because he has the feeling that he doesn't have a chance anyway; lets himself be roped into things for someone else's benefit against his own convictions.
- Lives in constant fear of punishment and is therefore also dishonest with himself and others.
- Suppresses his wishes and needs in favor of others; lives a falsely understood "love" that is willing to make sacrifices.

- Doesn't look at what he wants; gives too much because he can't say "no," can't draw lines; but also can't accept anything from others; wants to buy love for himself through gifts.
- Sees love as something pink, lulling and dulling to lavish upon others; believes that a person must swallow everything when he loves someone else.
- Feels himself to be unloved, alone, abandoned, and betrayed.
- Has unsolved problems related to his father.

But also a person who:
- Lives exaggerated authority; wants to force his will and viewpoints on others; doesn't listen to others.
- Lives power as manipulation and is on a power trip.
- Exercises power in order to rule over others but believes he's acting "for the other person's good" because he considers other people to be immature.
- Has lost the feeling for others; only acts in accordance with his own values, which he sees as right; has "eaten the truth with a spoon" and is convinced of his own truth, applying it to other people without any consideration.
- Is "hard."
- Feels himself misunderstood by the world when others don't accept his viewpoints.

The difference between No. 5—Christ and No. 6—Djwal Khul on the theme of "power and strength"

No. 5   develops power and leadership qualities on the basis of love and responsibility for the whole.

No. 6   includes one's own strength and promotes its use.

Description

The energy of Christ consciousness means the *Christ* energy and not the historical Jesus about whom the Bible tells us. In as far as I have learned through channeling sessions, the person of Jesus, of whom the Bible speaks, was led by Christ consciousness and ultimately dissolved his ego-Jesus definition in order to merge with the Christ consciousness (see Chapter 3 "The Life-work" for explanation). We can clearly recognize the *Christ* energy in the life of Jesus and experience to which path it leads. The outstanding themes of divine love or the love of the father, becoming conscious, and living the truth (even if it brings unpleasant consequences) therefore also applied to Jesus. For this reason, some of Jesus' saying are stated here as examples of the *Christ* energy.

All-encompassing love is shown in the love we have for other people, for our neighbors, for the people we encounter every day. And it is shown in our love of the earth, for the plants, animals, minerals, and water—simply for all of being. All-encompassing love can't be abstract. I can't say that "I love God" and fight against people and destroy the earth. Divine energy is within every human being. It is the essence of all being. Loving God means loving what he has created. The love of God is the love of all being. Jesus expressed it in this way: "...as you did it to one of the least of these my brethren, you did it to me." And Jesus' love for human beings was so great that he himself even was understanding of them on the cross: "Father, forgive them; for they know not what they do." He knows that people are in a deep sleep, that they are so busy with their egos that they can't see the solidarity and truth. We believe that we are separated from the whole. We believe that our will is different from "God's will," and we act on the basis of this condition. Yet, at the same time we find ourselves on the path of perception, and we are loved and accepted by the whole, connected with the entire existence.

Many people who work with this energy have told of a warm feeling: they felt themselves accepted, accompanied, and supported, as if someone walked at their side. They were strengthened in their situation.

The love of the Christ consciousness is clear and direct. It doesn't lull, obscure, swallow everything, and say "yes" to everything. The greater correlation, the divine source, can be perceived within it. Out of his love of God and human beings, Jesus drove the dealers out of the temple and argued with the Pharisees. This energy lets us clearly see and perceive, leading us to our own truth, which is ultimately identical with the universal truth. However, there may be intermediate stages on this path that we can't skip over. On this path we will have to confront others since they are at a different place that we ourselves. And these confrontations can take place in a clear and respectful way. "I accept you in your being and with your truth. I respect myself in my truth, but don't try to force your truth on me."

The *Christ* energy helps us perceive and examine our own truth time and again: "Does what I do correspond with my own truth?" This can leads to conflicts when the surrounding world doesn't accept changes in a person's behavior.

A woman who was working with the *Christ* energy began to carry out the conflicts with her husband and her mother-in-law that she had been putting off for years. She had fit herself into the family structures and increasingly set aside her own desires and needs in the process. Once she started to pay attention to herself and go her own way, she met with resistance.

It isn't necessary to achieve one's own truth through confrontations and battles. The *Christ* energy lets us also perceive different ways in which we can impart our truth so that others understand it. However, understanding doesn't imply the same thing as "always having to swallow everything." Which means that confrontations may happen. Yet, the goal should not be to win the conflict or to be proved right, but rather mutual understanding and respect. To do this, it is necessary to also see and accept the other person in his situation, to exchange experiences with each other, and to listen to the other person. Sometimes an exchange can be like a cleansing storm. Sometimes we must accept that we don't agree at the moment and there is no mutual solution.

This energy has a supportive effect in processes of finding oneself, as well as in the search for the self during puberty. These are times in which we scrutinize and examine old beliefs and society's viewpoints.

We need strength and love in order to attain self-knowledge so that we also look at and integrate our shadow aspects. Only then can we become healed and be in the full stream of vital energy and life's power.

The path of self-knowledge also has phases of doubt—times in which we no longer trust our perception and feel ourselves to be without orientation, in which we quarrel and ask ourselves whether we can really depend on help from the subtle world. Jesus also went through these processes, in the Garden of Gethsemane, for example. They are part of the path and ultimately strengthen our knowledge.

The essence makes us conscious of unsolved authority and father problems.

Through it, people who want to develop leadership qualities are also given support. True leadership acts in harmony with the cosmic law and with love. It is clear and understandable, acting for the benefit of the whole and for that of the individual human being. This means that we don't pass the bottle with alcohol to an alcoholic during withdrawal because he suffers and begs for it.

A true leader has a strong aura and charism, accepts criticism, contradictions, and help from others. Such people follow their own truth and are willing to examine it over and over again, orienting themselves to the whole. As a result, they can't be roped into doing something for someone else's benefit if they don't want to do it on their own.

True leadership is founded on love. Leadership without love is compulsion, and strength without love is violence. This makes the *Christ* energy a trailblazer for accepting one's own strength, for No. 6—*Djwal Khul.*

The theme of the *Christ* energy is also "taking and giving," two aspects of the same energy. Those who can't take also can't truly give on the basis of love. Some people believe that they are only permitted to accept something when they have done something or given something for it in return. And some people want to buy themselves affection and belonging through gifts to others. This often occurs unconsciously. When we work with the *Christ* energy, we become aware of the fundamental need for love and acceptance within us, and we develop the strength to take the necessary steps.

If the *Christ* oil is applied to the hand chakras, they open up. The energy flow of healing love is intensified. At the same time, the influx of this energy vibration is opened. This quality supports body workers and people who are often in contact with the sick because their own life energy *doesn't* flow away as a result.

Since sick people have a low energy potential, the health person's life energy flows towards them. After some time, the healthy person often feels tired, exhausted, and drained himself unless his life energy is immediately restored afterwards.

When the *Christ* essence is applied to the heart chakra, it heals emotional wounds.

The Meditation

Either stand or sit down and let a white-golden halo of light that envelops you be created from your center. It originates in the middle of the second chakra within your body and begins to shine like the sun. It grows and becomes larger, continually expanding itself. While this sun and the halo of the sun's light grows, you can recognize where there are dark areas around you. You can warm up these areas and dissolve them through the sun, through your own light-power. Some of them will simply disappear, and some will remain.

For the things that remain it is necessary that you consciously look at them, accept them, and lovingly take them into your arms.

Let this halo of light grow beyond your body into all the layers of your aura.

Let this halo of light grow a bit more every day.

After the meditation, reduce the halo of light to a size that is right for you until you one day go out into the world with your completely radiant light.

While the light shines through you, let yourself be healed by your own power, accept yourself, and warm yourself with your own divinity, feeling the connection with all being and with the highest being, with God or whatever you call this highest being.

Stay in this light as long as you like and draw strength from it for the new day or for the night. You can use it like a shower—in the morning to energize yourself and in the evening to cleanse yourself. Use it in between times for a change. When you have the feeling that your own strength in your center isn't adequate in order to enlighten yourself, then also call on the *Christ* energy for help.

The Message

I greet you and send you clarity and truth and the cosmic, divine, unconditional love that heals everything, dissolves and transforms what is old, leading you to fulfillment and your purpose. Love is the key to everything. Love connects and heals and lets you grow. Love is everything. It is like the ground, the plants, the fertilizer, and the rain. It includes everything, and it is the essence of all being.

By sending you this energy and supporting you, I teach you to accept yourselves with your mistakes and weaknesses, with your strengths and your divinity. I teach you to grow on the path of love, which accompanies you through the heights and the depths. It shows you beauty, the beauty of the heights and the beauty of the depths of life. It is with you and holds your hand. It is within you and makes up the core of your being. This is the love that is so often misunderstood by human beings, which is connected with suffering and drama, which is connected with power and the abuse of power. It is a love that in reality opens and connects and lets you be one with all of being and lets you perceive your true existence. This energy will also support you in perceiving yourselves and your true being, in seeing your truth and living in this truth, strongly standing up for it and going beyond all the old, negative experiences and fears, recognizing that truth and love are one.

And my energy will often be like an embrace, like the feeling of being accepted, like a child who has come home and is lovingly welcomed, knowing at the same time that it must still grow and grow and that it wants to do this and will do it.

So I teach you to perceive true love, the reason for all being, the origin, and the source. I teach you to be in truth and clarity, to lovingly accept yourselves and see the world with loving eyes—eyes that are not obscured and wear pink glasses, but that also clearly recognize and see, understand and accept the higher correlations.

No. 6—*Djwal Khul*

Accepting Your Own Strength

The Effect of the Master Essence

This essence helps in seeing and accepting one's own strength, power, and might.

- It strengthens the hara and the aura.
- It supports us in assuming responsibility for our own life.
- It helps us see where our own strength is blocked and that every individual shapes his own life, including even the blows of fortune.

Associated with the chakras: Solar plexus chakra (throat chakra)
Color: Green (emerald green)
Tarot card: No. 16—The Tower
Gemstone: Dioptase, moldavite
Oil application: Back and front of solar plexus chakra, between the shoulder blades, and upper arms (biceps area)

A person who has balanced this aspect:

- Knows his own strength and power and lives it without having to demonstrate it to the outside world ("It doesn't bother a tree when a wild boar rubs against it").
- Takes action on the basis of an inner strength, from the knowledge of having enough power to live through difficulties and obstacles.
- Has stamina, certitude, self-assurance, and self-confidence ("I am and I can!"); has the certainty of being able to master difficulties.
- Has imperturbable confidence despite difficult circumstances.
- Uses his strength to attain and manifest what he wants to achieve; acts in love and harmony while doing so, not in violence.
- Has connected his power with wisdom and love.

- Has an inner peace based on inner strength; is comparable with a powerful tiger that can be relaxed and calm because it knows that it can mobilize a great deal of energy at any moment; is both awake and attentive.

A person who has not yet balanced this aspect:
- Feels himself to be a victim: "I'm too weak, I can't do anything, the others are stronger, I can't, this always happens and will always happen to me, I don't have a chance." These are typical phrases for this state of mind.
- Has a lack of self-confidence: "I can't do that, I don't have any stamina because I'm too weak."; gives up quickly and fundamentally expects setbacks.
- Has his life lived by other people because he lets them do anything they want with him.
- Bears a grudge against fate; feels himself not responsible for his own position in life; the others are always at fault; feels himself helplessly at the mercy of others; experiences himself to be powerless.
- Looks for blame outside himself, in other people, in the society, and/or in the evil world.
- Has strong projections.
- Doesn't even give any thought to his own life; has no idea of it since he thinks he doesn't have a chance anyway.
- Has the desire to live in an intact world and be taken care of; wants to pass on responsibility like a child; complains about the evils of this world "but there's nothing we can do about it."

But also a person who:
- Has a dominating appearance and demonstrates his strength in order to show others how strong he is (because of his self-doubt and need to constantly prove that he has strength).
- Becomes a perpetrator because of his fear of becoming victim.
- Is always ready to attack and engage in conflict because he inwardly believes he is too weak and wants to prove to the surround world or himself that he is strong.

The difference between No. 6—Djwal Khul and No. 20—Aeolus on the theme of "being a victim":

No. 6   strengthens particularly when a person believes he is too weak to have any strength of his own; intensifies the belief in one's own power.

No. 20   strengthens particularly when a person believes he is at the mercy of the great totality; intensifies power on the basis of being connected with the whole.

The difference between No. 6—Djwal Khul and No. 5—Christ on the theme of "power and strength":

No. 6   includes an individual's own strength and gives support in applying it.

No. 5   develops power and leadership qualities based on love and responsibility towards the whole.

Description

Djwal Khul is the master who opens our eyes for our own power and strength.

It is often much more comfortable for us to be the victim and make others or the world responsible for how we are doing.

It is simpler to feel helpless, powerless, and at the mercy of the world, believing that we can't do what we want and forcing others to do something for us. "I can't" and "Why does this always happen to me?" are typical sentences for "victims."

How much easier is it to complain and lament when we don't succeed at something, to look for the blame for our situation in others or in the society, to project shadow aspects on others, and then condemn or avoid these people!

The step to becoming the master of our own destiny starts with recognizing that we ourselves have the entire responsibility for our lives, for everything that we do, and for what happens. This isn't easy, and it takes a while to learn this. But only when we have taken this step and acknowledge our possibilities of shaping our lives, see our creative qualities, and open ourselves up to our abilities for shaping our lives do we receive increasing access to our true strength—a power that isn't limited but has a connection to the cosmic source of strength.

A man, who owns his own company, wound up in considerable financial difficulties during the time when he was using the essence. He had moved into a larger office with more costs and had lost his biggest client at the same time. However, instead of falling into a fear-filled paralysis, which he usually would have done in this situation, he immediately began to do intensified canvassing and quickly found new clients. He also made use of this change in order to approach the clients whose assignments he had found to be more enjoyable. He told of how he'd had fears and worries during the entire transitional phase, but hadn't fallen into despair like before. Instead, he always knew that he had enough strength to make it.

One further step is leaving behind the child's idea of an intact world and seeing that the world isn't intact and that we aren't whole. The world is our mirror. This world is a world of polarities and therefore torn in two. There is pleasant and unpleasant, suffering and joy, day and night, and light and shadow aspects that are within us as well. Our path of healing is specifically acknowledging and integrating this polarity, overcoming the polarity, and once again becoming whole and healed.

With his powerful energy, Djwal Khul shows us where we deny our strength, where we don't want to assume responsibility. He makes us aware of our blocks and dissolves them, which may have an unsettling effect. It isn't easy to acknowledge that we have also created our own blows of fortune. He shows us the correlations between ourselves and what happens in our lives.

At the same time, he makes us aware of our own strength. He connects us with the power of our hara, lets us experience it, and opens the access to the cosmic source of strength. This is a strong transformation, and the result of it is self-assurance and self-confidence—"I am and I can." People who learn to accept this experience as inner peace based on the knowledge of their own strength, comparable with that of a powerful tiger that can be relaxed and calm because it knows it can mobilize a great deal of energy at any given moment. An individual who has power can afford to be calm, relaxed, and supremely confident. And he will have stamina.

A person who uses the essence can perceive that true strength can only be lived in connection with love and in connection with the entire being. This is why *Christ* precedes the energy of *Djwal Khul*. The essence opens and intensifies the connection between the solar plexus chakra and the heart chakra. Heart energies also can't truly be lived when they are feeble.

Djwal Khul then teaches us how to deal with power and strength so that we don't become tyrants who abuse power. People who constantly have to prove their power to others usually have doubts about it themselves.

The confrontation with this theme is important in our Western society. Many of us live in images of being victims with the feeling of being helpless and powerless. People who have completely assumed the responsibility for themselves and their lives, and live out their potential, are rare. We consider them to be exceptions. We believe that we ourselves are too weak, that we have to show consideration and cannot really live out who we are. Those who become involved with this energy may initially encounter many blocks that can also be expressed in the form of fatigue, exhaustion, and apathy.

The *Djwal Khul* energy has the color green, the green that we find in the power of nature. It is the power of the seed that becomes a tree, the power of the grass plant that pushes up through the concrete, and the power of the ivy that climbs up the house walls. Nature overcomes blocks and develops its potential to its full extent. We can learn from it.

The Meditation

Become a rock, a mountain, and if you can, become the Himalayas. Begin with smaller mountains—you don't have to start directly with the Himalayas. Then begin to feel what power and strength signify, what it means to stretch down deep into the earth and stand in one place, to be strong and powerful, towering into the highest heights, feeling how trees grow on the surface and their roots penetrate just a bit, how sometimes people and animals wander around on you. Feel how these people climb you to your peak and believe that they have conquered you.

Sense that there is no need to prove to these people that they have not conquered you. Feel that there is no need to prove and demonstrate your power and your strength to anyone at all. And even if avalanches of stones or snow crash down your slopes—it is a process that takes place on the surface but doesn't touch you on the inside. You watch, you let it happen, and you see the effects.

Even if you are covered with green as a mountain up to the peak and a wonderful vegetation grows on you and the work of human beings destroys it all, even then there will be no necessity of demonstrating your power. You survive all the change, you have withstood ice ages, you were there long before there was vegetation, and you will be there long after the vegetation is gone.

What happens in the course of a few years has another meaning for you because you live in greater dimensions.

And yet, you experience the sunrise and the sunset every day, and each day is still a new day for you.

Learn to be aware of each day, to live in every minute, and to still know that time does not exist.

Important: After the meditation, dance and come alive once again. Don't stay in the feeling of being a rock since this is not your nature. It only illustrates one aspect of power and strength that does not call for deeds and actions. This is why it is very important to become a lively human being again at the end, to become a child who dances and jumps for joy because of its liveliness and life to cheerful music. Dance in a boisterous and cheerful way for at least five minutes after the meditation and once again become alive.

The Message

I teach you to accept and use the power that you human beings possess in love. You all have more power and strength than you want to see. Your inner power and strength is truly boundless. As soon as you open yourselves, you will be connected to a power reservoir on another level. And truly unlimited energy flows there, even if you cannot imagine this with your limited minds.

My essence, my vibration will bring people in contact with might, with their own strength and power. It teaches you to assume responsibility for your lives, to be clear and clearly perceive, and to clearly see your own abilities.

I will thoroughly shake people up, just as you have been shaken up and like some others have been shaken up who have worked with my energy. At the end of this process, there will be a bit more divinity, a bit more clarity, and a bit more of the quality of being a creator.

So I teach you to accept your own creative power, to perceive and accept and see how it has been unconsciously used up to now and how it can be consciously used in the future.

I also teach you to lovingly accept yourselves after you have gone through a process since true power can only be lived in connection with the heart and with love. This is why I follow *Christ*, who teaches the truth and divine love. And only when the heart has opened can you deal with power and strength.

No. 7—Sanat Kumara

Connecting Heaven and Earth

The Effect of the Master Essence

This essence forms the bridge between heaven and earth, between the cosmic and earthly aspects of consciousness, and lets the divine portion be perceived in everything that is worldly.

It opens us for the energy of the earth and the cosmos, letting the earth energy flow through the crown chakra and the cosmic energy through the foot chakra, which connects the 1st and 7th chakras.

It allows us to understand the meaning of life on earth and make friends with life on the earth.

It helps us accept duality as a learning step.

We can become conscious of the themes related to father and mother and healed of them through the essence. The masculine and feminine principles are brought into balance.

Associated with the chakras: All
Color: Orange (yellow-orange)
Tarot card: No. 7—The Chariot
Gemstone: Chrysocolla
Oil application: 1st and 7th chakra and 7th cervical vertebra, as well as on the shoulders when they are tense

A person who has balanced this aspect:
- Enjoys living on the earth; is conscious of his divine aspects and likes to live on the earth.
- Lives in love of the material world and earthly things.
- Makes himself at home on the earth, both in the figurative sense—life is designed in a pleasant way—as well as in the concrete sense—the home and the work environment are furnished comfortably.
- Sees duality and sexuality as a path to unity.

145

A person who has not yet balanced this aspect:
- Has a deep longing for the "heavenly" realms; doesn't like to live on the earth and in duality; longs for unity, for paradise, and doesn't get involved in life or only by way of necessity; avoids learning steps.
- Feels life on earth to be bleak, hard, and a burden.
- Has tense shoulders from the earthly burden that he bears.
- Lives in disorderly, chaotic, oppressive circumstances; doesn't take care of his surroundings but lets them fall apart; places no value on earthly things.
- Has a longing for death in extreme cases.
- Doesn't want to see earthly things but constantly looks into other areas; has his gaze fixed on the heavens.
- Spends a great deal of time with dreaming as a flight from earthly reality.
- Doesn't live his abilities because he finds this to be a waste; prefers to withhold them.
- Has visions and ideas that appear to come from other dimensions but don't fit here on earth and can't be integrated; the visions are often not understood.
- Feels himself to be a creature from another world.
- Rejects duality, as well as sexuality, because it arises from the tension between the two poles; believes he will find healing in celibacy, in the rejection of the duality.

But also a person who:
- Is very earthy, avoids the themes of sexuality, doesn't want to confront thoughts of his own divinity; has a hard time accepting his divine aspect since he finds no access to it.
- Has a great potential and unusual ideas but can't translate them into action because they don't fit into his narrow earthly view of the world.

The difference between No. 7—Sanat Kumara, No. 11—Kuthumi and No. 13—Seraphis Bey:

No. 7 forms a bridge between heaven and earth, is a first contact with the earth.

No. 11 opens the connection to the earth, lets friendship be established with the earth.

No. 13 leads into the middle of the material world and brings consciousness into it.

Description

Sanat Kumara is the teacher of the earth. He teaches us to consciously bring our own divine aspect of being to the earth and into the material world. He is therefore a help for those people who long for "paradise in heaven, outside of the earth" to accept the earth as their home. He supports people who don't like to live on the earth, consider life on the earth to be difficult and oppressive, a burden on their shoulders, and therefore often have tensed shoulders and a general sense of tension. These people frequently feel a deep sadness and longing within themselves, as if they were far away from home at a place that they don't like and aren't there voluntarily. Sometimes this yearning goes as far as a death wish. For them, the feeling of "coming home" and once again being in the warmth and safety that we cannot find on the earth is connected with death—so they believe. When these people talk about such feelings with others they usually aren't understood. They are asked "Why are you so sad?" and "Where do you want to go?", but can't answer these questions.

Their surroundings and their bodies aren't important to them. They give little care to their body and material things are unimportant to them. Their living space is usually furnished very spartanically and not very comfortably. There are seldom pictures hanging on the walls, and they are concerned with always just owning the absolute necessities instead of too many things.

These people are usually suffering a shock that made them painfully aware of the difference between their origins and life on earth during the phase of pregnancy, birth, or during the early years of life. Instead of working on this separation, instead of taking the path of the seeker who wants to achieve unity on this earth, they withdraw. They often spend hours in meditation or dreams and then are sad afterwards because they have to return to the "real world" again and dedicate themselves to unloved tasks.

One woman who used this essence felt herself supported by it as she began to get a grip on her "earthly life." Before, she had kept herself afloat with various jobs and had become increasingly dissatisfied with her situation. As compensation, she had sat at the window for hours and daydreamed. When she took the essence, she asked herself what she wants in this life and what makes life on earth pleasant for her. She found ways of earning more money with work that she enjoyed. She moved into a more pleasant apartment.

Sanat Kumara opens our eyes to the idea that we ourselves have chosen life on the earth, that we have chosen the duality in order to once again find the path to unity and grow in consciousness as we do so. But this doesn't happen by our fleeing from the earth since we could have stayed where we were in that case. Instead, we do this by developing and living out our divine aspect on the earth. By increasingly recognizing our true inner being and feeling good here on the earth, we recognize the earth as the place we have chosen to temporarily be our home. He helps us find the way to accept the duality and love it. We recognize our own path in life, accept, respect, and love the earth with all its creatures and objects, and accept ourselves and our body. Then we are also willing to contribute our abilities, our potential that we had previously held back. Sanat Kumara helps us to accept the earth as our homeland and recognize the beauty of this place.

As we started to work with Sanat Kumara, we improved our apartment and furnished it in a comfortable way. Although we had already lived in it for more than a year, some of the moving cartons still hadn't been unpacked. There weren't enough closets, some rooms hadn't been completely furnished, our pictures were all still packed in the cellar, and naked light bulbs hung from the ceilings in some of the rooms. All of this hadn't been important to us before.

The same thing happened to a girlfriend who had just moved and, following her initial enthusiasm, had lost her desire to finish decorating her new apartment. After she had started taking the Sanat Kumara essence, she completely furnished the place in one weekend, unpacked the last cartons, and hung up the pictures.

With *Sanat Kumara* I began to enjoy being on the earth, started loving life on the earth, and was happy to be here and have a body.

Sanat Kumara is the bridge, the initial friendly contact with life on the earth. When we have accepted the place earth, *Kuthumi* strengthens the connection to the earth energy and brings us a bit more into the earthly world so that *Seraphis Bey* can then completely bring our consciousness into our earthly body, into the earthly power, and into the middle of the material world. Our earthly aspect is then imbued with our divine being.

However, this sequence of energies doesn't mean that people who have problems with the earth should begin by using the *Sanat Kumara* essence. In order to find out which essence offers the best support, you should trust your intuition or do a test using an appropriate procedure.

The *Sanat Kumara* essence intensifies the flow of cosmic energies, as well as the earth energy. As a result, we attain more grounding and a stronger connection to our body. At the same time, our spiritual abilities grow. We become just like a tree that is rooted deep within the earth and can even form a larger crown without losing its equilibrium.

One man who worked with this essence discovered that he has access to the higher state of consciousness. Although he had always had unusual ideas, he hadn't translated them into action because that hadn't fit into his view of the world and his life. Although he was successful in earthly life, he often felt unfulfilled and cut off from things. Through the essence, he was able to connect both aspects and recognized how he could translate his ideas into reality.

If you apply the oil to your shoulders, you will often notice how the shoulders drop downwards, as if someone had taken a load off of them. When we perceive that this life on earth doesn't have to be a burden but can also be fun, we can then loosen up our shoulders and be more relaxed in life.

Sexuality is also an expression of duality and of being separated from the unity, from God. This is why some religions also attempt to return to the unity by denying or overcoming sexuality.

However, we cannot go beyond duality and sexuality by rejecting and excluding them—instead, we continue to be bound up in them.

Sexuality and sensuality is a theme in which duality is particularly strongly expressed. This is precisely where a conscious confrontation with this theme may take place. Individuals who accept the polarity of sexuality can unite and merge into an orgiastic unity.

Heaven and earth also symbolize the masculine and feminine principles, which makes them symbols of sexuality as well. Through the essence, we can heal the wounds of our own masculine and feminine aspects, as well as themes regarding father and mother. It creates an equilibrium between the poles.

The Meditation

Imagine that you are lying in a meadow. Shape this image so that it pleases you—with plants and flowers and blossoms, perhaps with trees at the edge or in the meadow. If you like, imagine that animals are in the meadow: deer, cows, and insects. Look at the sky. See the green around you and the colorful splendor of the flowers. Take in everything that belongs to the earth and is important for you. You can also make contact with the beings who are connected with the earth—the fairies and elves, the gnomes and mandrakes, and whatever else you encounter there. Go completely into this image.

Then begin to merge with the earth's forms of being. Become the blade of grass, the butterfly, the cow that stands in the meadow and chews, become an earthworm, the ground from which the grass grows, become a stream and the water that flows through the meadow, become the clouds that move across the sky, the air that surrounds everything, or a tree. Stretch your roots deep into the earth and your leaves high up into the heavens and so on.

Don't do all of this on one day. Choose specific themes for yourself or observe what attracts you during meditation—one or two things that you then become. And pay very precise attention to your perceptions, to what you feel and sense as a blade of grass, what you see and how you perceive the world, what you think about it, how connected you are with it and the other plants, with human beings, what you are made of, and what your life as a blade of grass means. Experience all of this.

Also experience the mountains, the ocean, the deepest depths of the deep sea, and the highest peak of the mountains. Become a plant that grows on the mountain, become a continent, and finally, after you have done this meditation for quite some time, become the earth. Connect yourself with the entity of the earth and feel what it feels, sense what it senses, perceive what it perceives—how it sees itself in the universe, how it looks to the outside, how it travels its course, sees the sun, and whether it has contact with the other planets. And also notice what happens on it and within it, how it is to be covered with land and sea, to be robbed, contaminated, and poisoned, to give birth to animals and human beings—and to once again let them pass away, to create stones and plants, mountains and rivers—and to let them pass away again.

Notice how it is to be in connection with human beings and perceive the positive and negative experiences. Become the earth and learn to understand it. Then, at the end of the mediation, thank it for what it has done for you, for the body it has given you, for the food that keeps you alive, for the energy that it gives you every day. Thank it and send it your light or your love. Strengthen it and support it. Accompany it on its way. Give it what you would like to give it.

This is the end of the meditation.

The Message

My message is: Love the earth with everything that belongs to it. Love your body—it is the mirror of the earth, the microcosm within the macrocosm. My message is the love of material being.

I am the teacher of the earth, the teacher of humanity, and I teach you the love of all being on the earth, of what you call animate nature and inanimate nature. Even inanimate existence is animate in its own form.

I am the teacher of the earth and also of the dawning Age of Aquarius with some of my other friends among the Ascended Masters. I, *Sanat Kumara*, teach human beings to get back in touch and to be with the earth. I teach them to love their bodies and love the earth with all its forms of being—animals, plants, stones, and everything there is. This includes not only the natural forms of being, but also the forms of existence created by humans—machines like dishwashers, cars, and toothbrushes since every thing is made from the material of the earth. It has been processed from it.

With what right do you give a picture painted by an artist more attention and more love than a toothbrush, which has also been created by a human being and is also made of material. Start to respect and honor the things that surround you, and also honor and love your bodies since they make it possible for you to be here on this wonderful planet. It makes it possible for you to learn and grow in steps. It makes it possible for you to feel happiness and bliss and continue to develop yourself in a very specific way.

You can have experiences here on this planet that aren't possible anywhere else in this universe. The earth is unique in many respects, and so I enjoy being the teacher of the earth and send my energy to human beings so that they begin to love their bodies and the earth with all its forms of being—as well as respect and love the entity of the earth.

Become conscious of what you have learned here on the earth and what you want to learn. I support you on your path through this incarnation, and I support you in becoming clear about your goal, that you want to live here on the earth. Much clarity with regard to their own path here on earth will arise for people who surround themselves with my energy. I support you in attaining clarity in a great diversity of areas in life so that you can live from the depths of your hearts and with love, respect for the gifts that you receive, and respect for the earth.

I support you in your incarnation on the earth, and I also support the entity of the earth because I am responsible for the entire planet in order to increase the consciousness here. Everything is linked with everything else, and when the consciousness of humanity increases, the entity of the earth grows as well. You can mutually support each other by feeling your love for the earth, feeling yourselves connected, and loving your bodies, which are gifts from Mother Earth.

During the age of matriarchal cultures, this was an obvious idea. The people had a strong connection with the earth, which is why it was also called "Mother." In the coming age, it is important to recreate this connection. It was lost during the patriarchal period, but this was also an important learning step on your paths. So don't evaluate this age negatively. As a result of it, things have been created and have come about that wouldn't have been here without it. The many inventions and tools that you own and the numerous technologies wouldn't exist without the age of patriarchy. *So everything is alright.*

The next step is to connect to the two aspects. Since you find yourselves in an age of patriarchy, it is important to once again love the earth, remain connected with it, and use it in a loving way. You can also apply the energies of the earth for your own personal development and for the creation of material things. If you do this in harmony with the earth, many things will turn out better and not harm the earth. You should therefore learn what it means to love the earth, to be here on this earth, to develop yourselves in a body of your own, and also accept and love this body as a gift of the earth. You should also learn to prepare the earth's path for its own development. This is also a part of your task. As the teacher for the earth, I therefore connect your souls, the subtle cosmic energies, with the earth, the material energies. When people work with this energy, they will attain a strong connection and begin to love the earth.

No. 8—*Angelica*

Transformation of the Past

The Effect of the Master Essence

The essence of *Angelica* lets us perceive that negative experiences are learning steps that haven't been taken, that experiences are completed through step-by-step learning. It takes the emotional encumbrances from the memories and the past attains the proper degree of importance. We learn from it, but don't cling to it. The experiences of the past are used for our further development.

It supports the healing of dreams from the past, even from past lives.

Through the transformation of the past, we open up the access to our own potential.

It helps us in every type of learning, evaluating, and drawing conclusions.

It supports every process of working through the past and also opens the access in therapies like reincarnation therapy.

When the body's problem zones are massaged with *Angelica* Oil, we can become conscious of the experiences stored there and transform them.

Associated with the chakras: Sacral chakra (throat chakra)
Color: Pink
Tarot card: No. 13—Death
Gemstone: Labradorite, rhodochrosite
Oil application: Throat, to the side of the larynx, from the chin to the collarbone, on the sacral chakra (2 fingers below the navel); additionally on the forehead chakra

A person who has balanced this aspect:
- Understands his own history, his own path in life.
- Has comprehended that one cannot run from the past; when suppressed, it just becomes invisible.

- Stands in direct contact with the past and puts the experiences of the past to use.
- Sees and uses the past as a part of his own history, his own path of development.
- Gives thought to conspicuous situations and the course of the day in order to learn from it.
- Doesn't repeat mistakes; sees mistakes as learning steps and valuable experiences.

A person who has not yet balanced this aspect:

- Suppresses the past and his dreams of the past; doesn't remember or doesn't like to remember; avoids coming to terms with the past.
- Doesn't see the connection between the past and his current situation in life.
- Buries himself in the past, focussing on nothing else but the past; usually just remembers the "good old times"; believes that everything was better in the old days; clings to positive memories and loses his perspective of the present; or just lives in the future.
- Has mentally gotten caught in the past; sentences like "I used to..." or "When I was still..." illustrate this state and show that the past hasn't been properly digested yet.
- Always goes through the same mistake because he doesn't learn from the past and doesn't look back.
- Always starts something new without looking to see why the old things went wrong; doesn't profit from experiences of the past.
- Doesn't look at his own patterns and thought structures.
- Is afraid of the unconscious mind, of memories and images that could arise from the unconscious.

The difference between No. 8—Angelica and No. 15—St. Germain on the theme of "the past":

No. 8   heals through transformation.

No. 15   frees through understanding and lets the deeper correlations be perceived; new perspectives arise as a result.

Description

The theme of "the past" is a topic that people approach in a great variety of ways. Some people live in their memories and forget that there is still life in the present. Others want nothing more to do with the past, they suppress it or want to get rid of it as quickly as possible. The past is seldom used as a reservoir of experiences that we can fall back upon when we have freed them of the emotional burdens clinging to them. The cleansing of emotional burdens and the healing of old wounds is called transformation. As a result, the experiences become available and the treasures of the past can be put to use after they have been freed from the clinging dust.

The *Angelica* energy lends support precisely in this situation. She helps us perceive ourselves, comprehend our own history, and thereby be able to newly define ourselves in the present.

She frees the past from valuations so that it can be seen as what it is: learning experiences that we can use. When we evaluate the past as "good," there is the danger of not letting go of it, getting stuck in memories, and not being free to look at the present. If we call it "bad," we tend to suppress it. Then it sinks down into the unconscious mind and we keep it behind a door there so that we don't have to look at it again.

Holding this door shut costs energy that we need in other places—and suppressed memories have the tendency of turning into monsters. Whatever we desperately try to keep in the dark appears much larger, more dangerous, and worse than it was or actually is. We are afraid that if it ever came to light, it would overpower us. However, it becomes manageable if we dare to take a look at it. *Angelica* helps in slowly opening such doors and healing the old wounds. As a result, more energy becomes available again. We have greater strength and joy in life, and an inner peace is created.

Angelica also frees us from the valuation of the present. Things that we don't want to see in the present and mentally fade out because they are unpleasant for us develop into the suppressed burden of the past. By looking at them, we can perceive the learning experiences before they appear in very distinct terms— as an illness, for example. We become free of bogged-down patterns of behavior, beliefs, and imprints and can behave differently in the future.

Transformation of the past doesn't mean getting rid of everything and resolving it as quickly as possible. Some experiences to which we have no access also have an important function in the present of our life and are still needed. Then it isn't the right time at the moment to transform them. Unpleasant experiences that we have had can, for example, take on a protective function. They have so sensitized us that we are (unconsciously) very vigilant about not getting caught in such a situation again. As long as we are missing the basis for consciously avoiding such situations, the experience that is encumbered with negative feelings can't be worked through. Otherwise, its protective function would be set aside.

One example: A child has an unpleasant experience in the dark and is afraid at night of going out of the house alone in the dark. The fear of the dark can continue over many years without this person remembering the experience. For the child, this fear serves as protection and it is helpful for the child not to remember the experience, transform it, and then lose its fear of the dark. Only when it is an adult, has enough strength and vision to go out into the dark alone will the memory of the unpleasant experience be set free and can be resolved. The protective function of fear is no longer necessary.

It's important to treat yourself and past experiences in a loving way. Not only do they have their justification, but every experience contains an important learning step. It is a signpost towards unity that shows what we are lacking and what we still must integrate. A person who takes a loving look at the past can consciously decide which parts he would like to transform or dissolve, where he wants to take new paths, and what parts he isn't ready to let go of yet.

However, loving acceptance isn't always easy. The following image may help in illustrating this point: You see the old things that rise up to the top from the unconscious mind, like the dark piece of a puzzle that is missing in the overall picture. Instead of being black, it is unlit. Without this little piece, the picture cannot become complete. When the light of understanding falls on this little piece of the puzzle, you can recognize what is depicted on the puzzle piece and to which part of the picture it belongs. Put the little piece in the right place of the overall picture. Through this exercise, it may happen that—after the one little piece has been put into its proper place—other dark pieces suddenly become light: the larger correlations can now be understood. Some other unpleasant experiences are transformed at the same time.

You can use this image as a meditation. When doing so, it is possible to use the abstract picture described here or use a concrete picture from the past as a "little piece of the puzzle."

The work with *Angelica* leads to a deep understanding of one's own path of development. We can understand the life goal for our momentary life and the situation on our path. We can see why we chose these parents, this history, these difficulties, and the blows of fate that we have experienced up to now. The essence makes it easier to look at the situations from a distance, from a different or higher perspective and detached from emotional entanglements. We understand and can accept things since it is ultimately our history that has brought us to the path of becoming conscious.

Through this energy, access is possible not only to experiences in this life, but also those that occurred during the prenatal period and in past lives. We have also created karma there, experiences that we didn't resolve and that have an effect on our current life and give rise to similar occurrences here as well (also see Chapter 3 "Past Lives").

However, the essence only allows access to the situations that are ripe for us and ready to be transformed.

People who use this essence report of intensive dreams during their sleep.

Working through the past for its own self makes little sense. It serves as the foundation for the present and the future, in order to trustingly go into the future. This is why *Angelica* precedes the *Orion* essence.

Abilities that we haven't yet used but have unconsciously blocked have their basis in the past. As a result, *Angelica* also helps us develop our potential. However, this happens slowly. If we could throw away all our blocks at one time, we would develop abilities with which we couldn't yet cope. We need a certain maturity for some abilities. A three-year-old child doesn't have

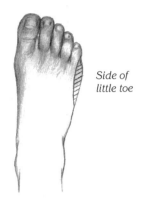

*Side of
little toe*

Zone for learning disorders (according to Peter Mandel)

the strength and muscle control to ride an Arabian mare and probably no one would give this child such an opportunity. The same applies to an inner wisdom within us that keeps the doors closed. We grow by overcoming the blocks and thereby attain the necessary preconditions for dealing with the abilities as they open up.

The blocks offer us a further means of protection. Some abilities that we bear within us would be destroyed if they became available too early. Children lose their clairvoyance because they can't yet classify these perceptions, because they learn that they aren't "right," because they are laughed at and don't have the strength and vision to defend themselves. If clairvoyance first develops during the age of adulthood, we can better understand and integrate it into our lives.

Sometimes healing is connected with sadness. Old patterns and limitations are very familiar to us, and we feel ourselves secure with them. The loss of something that has accompanied us for such a long time and supported us in its own way can be painful at first.

Angelica not only helps us learn from the past, but also supports every type of learning, evaluation of experiences, and drawing of conclusions. It also helps children with learning difficulties. The oil can be applied to the learning points (see illustration).

However, you should in any case first ask the child whether it wants the support of this essence. This applies particularly to children who usually have a good sense of what is right for them at the moment. If they don't want the essence, then there's a good reason for it that we perhaps don't recognize at the moment.

When the oil is applied to the problem zones of the body, it can dissolve the energies and resolve the experiences bound there and make us conscious of them. Healing is greatly supported when the meditation described below is done and we give thanks to the parts of the body during such work. Perhaps it also is possible to thank the places that cause pain and complaints. It's worth a try, even if the gratitude isn't meant seriously at the start.

A new phase in our work with the masters began with *Angelica*. I completed the job that I had done before and the "open construction sites," things that I had been putting off for a long time. Then my full energy directed itself towards the process with the masters.

A seminar that I had booked months before, in which I confronted the unresolved portions of my past, "coincidentally" took place during this time.

Among other things, I meet a man at this seminar who resembled someone with whom I had unfinished business. I had left back then without clarifying certain things. A part of the story repeated itself with the man at the seminar, and I was able to finish the things that had remained open at that time. Months later, I "coincidentally" encountered the first man, who I hadn't seen for two years. We no longer had much to say to each other or to clear up, so we hugged each other and separated in friendship after 5 minutes. I haven't encountered him since then.

The Meditation

Imagine that you are walking along a path through a lovely landscape and you are loaded down with a heavy backpack that contains your entire past. You don't know exactly what's in the backpack. You think that you're only dragging around needless stuff with you.

Then sit down at the edge of the path, perhaps on a stone, surrounded by a lovely landscape with the twitter of the birds and a stream flowing by. Open the backpack. You find many little packages that are wrapped up in many layers of paper. You can't see what's in them. Take one of them out of the backpack and start unwrapping it. Every layer of paper contains a piece of your history on a very specific theme.

You can choose the theme in advance and then unpack the corresponding object or you can simply reach in and see what images come up.

Remove the first layer of paper and experience parts of your past, perhaps as pictures of situations, perhaps as emotions or memories, however it feels right for you. You can then unwrap one layer after the other. You find feelings and memories from this life or perhaps even from the time before it.

The more you unpack, the clearer it becomes to you what a present you are holding in your hands. And every layer of paper that you remove brings you closer to the gift that is contained within it. The closer you come, the more clearly you recognize the valuable nature of the contents. Then, when you hold it in your hands, you perceive your unique ability and your potential that you have brought with you. Perhaps you also recognize how it is protected through the layers of paper. They have protected your precious potential from coming to light too early and being broken. The unwrapping of this potential, this quality, is your development. You go through many steps in order to be willing, to accept this precious thing, in order to be ready to deal with it and put it to use. You go through these steps in order to grow. And you can therefore accept both the paper and the precious thing within it.

At the end of the meditation you can choose whether you want to pack up this ability or quality once again and put it back into the backpack or whether you want to wear it on your body in order to let it take effect.

Then close the backpack and put it on again. Perhaps you notice how you now carry it with more love and joy. Although you don't yet know what the other packages contain, you do know that they hold something necessary for your journey. And so you continue on your way.

Repeat this meditation and unpack your backpack piece by piece, recognizing your abilities.

You will find more and more within it and recognize what abilities you have with increasing exactness.

The more you have unpacked, the more peaceful and quiet you will become inside yourself. You can more and more accept your history, the past, and the future. You find your way to the wisdom that: "Everything is good as it is—it is like it is." You come increasingly into the void, to inner peace and calm.

The Message

Looking at the past is one of the most important steps in the growth of a human being since the past is the ground and the seed from which you grow. Like a seed that has brought nutrients from the plant from which it comes along with it so that it can grow, you have also created your past for yourselves. And it is neither good nor bad. It was as it was, and it could have been different. But this is insignificant. You create your own learning steps, paths, and tasks that you want to master. And you also receive support in doing so.

In every moment of your lives you are creators, whether you are conscious of this or not. And the more conscious you become, the more clearly you will create your lives and grow so that you can take on other tasks. And when you accept the past and see it as something that was and that leads to where you are today, making it possible for you to walk your path—no matter whether you are at a point that you see as positive or negative—you are standing at a place in your lives from which you will continue, from which you will collect new experiences, and where you have already collected many experiences. Each point has its tasks, and you are in love, in the love of the divine and the love of yourselves, in every point. You are not alone because you are one with everything.

My energy can make you aware that the type of past you have chosen is not important. It could just as well been the past of your neighbor, your children, or your parents. Everything is a path, and everything leads to the same goal, to the *self*.

My energy supports the process of accepting yourselves with your past without any type of valuation.

No. 9—*Orion*

Visions

The Effect of the Master Essence

This essence opens the connection to the Higher Self and to the life plan. As a result, a person can more clearly see the visions for his own life. We become more trusting of our own intuition, our own inner voice.

It supports every type of therapeutic work that brings under-standing and structure into life, such as personal counselling.

It helps in every phase of reorientation and at the beginning and conclusion of projects.

It supports the inward journey.

Associated with the chakras: Forehead chakra (throat chakra)
Color: Light-blue
Tarot card: No. 12—The Hanged Man
Gemstone: Coelestine
Oil application: Crest of the ilium (upper edge of pelvic bone), third eye, medulla (back side of third eye), ishial tuberosity (buttock bones that we sit on)

A person who has balanced this aspect:
- Has visions for his own path in life that are in harmony with his life plan.
- Can let visions arise; has intuition.
- Takes an exact look at his own history; can see present, past, and future as a unity, as a line, and has a general overview as a result; shapes his life from his experiences and the pres-ence of the future.
- Has recognized that everything in life has a purpose, which gives his life structure.
- Sees the possibilities that are available to him; sees how many paths there are for achieving a goal without becoming fright-ened of them; can easily choose the path and knows that he

can change this choice time and again and that new possibilities will come up over and over again as well.
- Also has visions related to the larger correlations, such as the development of trends, the development of enterprises and projects, and the evolution of humanity.
- Perceives his own potential and develops it.

A person who has not yet balanced this aspect:
- Doesn't know where he wants to go; either has no goals or just vague, abstract objectives.
- Looks for paths for his life but can't make a decision because he doesn't know where he wants to go; the following sentence applies to him: "Whoever doesn't know the goal can't find the way to get there."
- Doesn't know how he should attain a set goal and what steps are necessary.
- Refuses to have visions.
- Gets stuck in working through his past; believes that he must cleanse himself time and again and continually work through the past because he can't imagine the future.
- Balks at the idea of setting goals because he is afraid of having to make a decision and thereby losing all the other possibilities.
- Acts without thinking beforehand.
- Starts new projects time and again; doesn't want to commit himself.
- Is afraid of predictions.
- Has no contact with the Higher Self.

But also a person who:
- Is an unrealistic dreamer.

Description

Popular wisdom teaches us that: "Whoever doesn't know the goal can't find the way to get there." And we have already experienced this often enough ourselves: The best abilities and the most extensive knowledge are worthless if we don't know what to use it for, just like the best tools are unusable if someone doesn't know what to do with them.

At the moment when we clearly see our goal, doors will open. We get clear ideas and encounter helpful information and supportive people. If, for example, we have made the decision to buy a new car and know the brand we want, we will suddenly see these cars everywhere we look. We will find an article about them in a magazine and acquaintances will talk to us about it. This information was naturally there beforehand, but we hadn't noticed it since the unconscious mind had categorized it as "unimportant" and filtered it out.

Even valuable advice and information are of no help to us without a goal. We don't know what we should do with it. Why is it often so difficult to decide what to do? This isn't because we don't know the future since we do shape the future with our decision. It is difficult for us because we don't know our goal. If we want to put together a puzzle without ever having seen the picture, we can spread out all the pieces in front of us but the decision where to put what is still difficult. However, in life there are pieces that don't even belong to the picture, mixed in with the puzzle pieces that do. Are you still wondering why you have such as hard time making decisions?

Orion will help you in this process of opening up to visions and goals.

One person who used the essence had been looking for a job for some time but couldn't find anything. After he had worked with the *Orion* energy, he became aware of the type of work he desired and what was important to him. A short time later, he found an appropriate position.

One woman who used them, the owner of a store in a larger city, had already been looking for a new apartment and the possibility of enlarging her store for the past six months. She began working with the *Orion* and the *Kamakura* essence at the same

165

time and within one week found her dream apartment with cheaper rent in the city. She was even offered a second appropriate apartment and found an office room located directly across from her store. This meant that she could also expand her store.

Through the essence, we open the channel to our Higher Self and get back into harmony with our plan in life. The results of this are long-term and short-term goals, as well as the means for attaining them. Now it is easier to make decisions.

There are always a number of paths that lead to the goal. Some people put themselves under pressure and block their ability to act because they believe that there is only one single correct way and that they must find it. If they take the wrong path, then everything is over or a great deal of time is lost through detours. Yet, life is like a buffet—there are many paths open to us and the individual paths are connected with each other. We can make a selection and, if we don't like the taste of the chosen path, we can go back to the buffet and chose something new. Perhaps the same paths that were there the first time are gone, but the new selection is just as good or as bad as before.

Orion supports us in seeing the lines in life, what we bring with us from the past, the state of things in the present, and where we want to go in the future. This applies to individual projects, the larger correlations in life, or even an entire lifetime. It applies to both the decisions of everyday life, as well as the fundamental decisions of life. And it also lets us see what blocks are in our way or those that we ourselves have placed on our path. These may be old patterns of behavior that we constantly repeat or beliefs that impede our success. We recognize which values are important to us since we can use them as guides and decision-making criteria when they are conscious. A further aspect of this is to also see what needs to be done so that the visions don't just stay dream castles but materialize in the here and now.

Some people are stuck in the past. They have cleansed the wounds of childhood, have reached past lives in this cleansing process, and still haven't made any significant progress. They wonder about this. If someone asks them where they are headed for, they have no idea. The cleansing of the past has become an end in itself. But the result is that the energies set free by the cleansing, which could flow into a new project or a positive vision, remain unused.

Some people find that these old things have become familiar and dear, which is why they don't look to the future. Change always has two aspects, namely finishing up the old and beginning the new. Those who find finishing things up to be a sad experience—since it always means saying farewell to something with which we are well acquainted and very familiar—fight against it and don't want to have something new that is unfamiliar.

Orion helps us to see this, keep going, and not get stuck in the old things. Life is a journey into uncertainty and into the unknown. Once we have accepted this, it is easier to take action.

For some people, using the *Orion* essence also opens up access to larger dimensions. They have visions for large projects, enterprises, businesses, companies, groups of people, the path of humanity, and the earth.

The Meditation

Imagine that you are standing in a valley at the foot of a mountain and look up to its peak, which you want to reach. You can give this peak a theme for which you desire to strive or want to achieve at the moment. Or just work with the image of the peak.

You are carrying a backpack that contains everything required for the trip. Yet, the backpack still feels light and pleasant.

Choose a path, a way of reaching the peak, and start the ascent. Sometimes stones lie on the path. Sometimes the path is blocked and you must find another way to get to where you're going. Or now and then you may have to go back a bit or change your route. There are places on your path that are completely beautiful, perhaps a mountain meadow with thousands of flowers in a great variety of colors, an enchanting scent, and twittering birds. Stay there for a while.

At other points you feel like you are heavy and oppressed, such as when you go through a dark forest or a ravine. Or you may cross scree that feels unsafe under your feet, making you afraid of triggering a landslide and being torn into the depths by it. You go through phases of fear, anger, despair, and helplessness. And then come phases of light and blissfulness, of joy and high spirits.

Continue on your path and approach the peak more and more. Take an exact look at the peak. Notice how many obstacles you have placed in your path, as well as how much joy and help it has held for you.

Be certain that you will reach the peak. Don't let your mind talk you into anything else. You will reach the peak if you want to. It's completely up to you.

Even in places where you sometimes think there is no path to follow, you still find a way—because you want to find it! For the first person to climb it, this is sometimes very difficult since he goes into the unknown. And yet, he succeeds even if he has to take a break at times or go back along the same path for a while. He reaches the peak.

Perhaps along the way he will decide to select another peak, another goal. Through the height that he has attained, he has achieved a better perspective of things. In the same way, you will experience over and over again that you can reach the goal that you want to attain.

At the end of the meditation, see yourself sitting on the peak and look back along the path that you have taken. Give yourself recognition for having continued on your path and having reached your goal despite the obstacles.

Be happy that you are in the expansiveness and stillness of the mountain peak and enjoy it.

The Message

I greet you and support you in obtaining a clear, wide view of your lives and in recognizing what steps are coming up for yourselves, and which paths you choose. I open your eyes not only for which path you choose but also for the variety that is possible on the earth and on your path. I teach you to receive visions that are in harmony with your life plan—visions that are in harmony with the universal truth, with the cosmic whole. It will be like a light on your path when you have the access and a connection to your Higher Self because so many things will be much easier for you. Then you will know what you have chosen and which paths lead there. And, in addition, you can see what life means for you.

When you have opened your door, it is also possible for you to see how you can shape life on the earth so that it is in harmony with the creative existence.

No. 10—*Kamakura*

Taking Action

The Effect of the Master Essence

This essence allows the energy to flow once again. Since it strongly energizes, *don't take it in the evening.*

As a result, much energy is available for work, which is then usually done more quickly than otherwise.

It helps us take action in a practical way.

It brings us enjoyment in our work, in acting, and in movement.

It helps us go beyond the blocks and fears of taking action.

It strengthens the "inner warrior."

The essence supports people who don't like the morning hours, who have a hard time getting up.

A combination of *Angelica, Orion,* and *Kamakura* is recommended for new projects and at the beginning of new phases of life.

This essence shouldn't be taken when a person has no idea of a goal or hasn't yet planned and ordered the steps he wants to take. Then it brings a desire for action that cannot be lived out.

It helps against jet lag. When arriving at a new place, a drop of oil on the third eye transports the body and soul directly into the here and now of the current location.

Associated with the chakras: Solar plexus chakra (base chakra)
Color: Green
Tarot card: No. 11—Strength (Lust)
Gemstone: Citrine
Oil application: Solar plexus, knee-caps, as well as along the spinal column from the coccyx to the cervical vertebra, shoulder blades

A person who has balanced this aspect:
- Takes his life into his own hands and does what he has planned to do.
- Reaches his goals; has the courage to tackle projects; has stamina.
- Has a positive attitude towards work.
- Doesn't let his fears dissuade him from taking action; can put his fears aside and try things out and do things.
- Learns by doing; recognizes what he still lacks, practices until he can do something well.
- Enjoys work, movement, and taking action.
- Has enough energy to reach his goals.
- Perceives when the time is right for taking action and when it's better for him to wait.

A person who has not yet balanced this aspect:
- Has many visions and new ideas constantly about what he could do but doesn't start anything and doesn't take any practical steps; postpones everything.
- Intends to do a great deal every day, achieves little, and is frustrated in the evening.
- Has the idea that he exhausts himself in taking action; would prefer to stay in bed, sleeps too much.
- Has an overfilled desk, yet continually puts the work off until the next day; instead, spends a long time planning how he can best carry out the work and the quickest way to master it.
- Has a tendency to escape into illness so that he has a reason for his lack of taking action.
- Collects knowledge, training, abilities; does increasingly more to improve himself but doesn't make practical use of this knowledge.
- Is afraid of doing something; is afraid of truly putting his physical powers to use and exhausting himself.
- Allows his fear to stop him from taking action.
- Lives his life with the "hand-brake" on.

The difference between No. 10—Kamakura and No. 4—Kwan Yin on the theme of "taking action":

No. 10   brings energy into the action, strengthens actively taking action at the right point in time, and helps overcome
fears. The transformation of fears occurs through positive experiences.

No. 4   tends to strengthen the passive side of taking action, the
ability to let things happen and doing something in harmony with the flow of life. We let go of fears and are
healed as a result.

Description

Visions are the spiritual form of reality. They "have an effect" in
the spiritual world, but not in the material world. *Kamakura* represents the step of bringing the mental forms to the earth.

Before any type of act takes place there is a thought, no matter whether we cook, tank the car, or manage a company. First
we think that we want to do something, then we take action.
This procedure is usually unconscious.

Kamakura brings us the joy of taking action, the joy of doing
something and being in action. It lets the energy flow once again
and allows us to act in practical terms. Planned actions that
have been postponed time and again are now translated into
reality. The inner dialog no longer obstructs the planned steps.
We start to do something.

The owner of a company had long planned to restructure his
business, but had never done it. When he began to work with
the *Kamakura* essence, he carried out his project within two weeks
and had the strength and the courage to implement far-reaching
changes. He was also more clear, assertive and straightforward
than before in negotiations and achieved his objectives.

Another person who used No. 10 began to tackle and translate into action all the things that he had already been putting off
for a long time. Although he had known exactly what he wanted
to do and should do, he had been lying in bed mornings and had
no desire to start work instead of buckling down. Through No.
10 he gained momentum and strength and within a short time
took care of all the work he had put off.

Blocks that had previously stopped us from doing something can be overcome. The energy flows once again so that we quickly feel ourselves strengthened and energized when we take this essence. Because of the strong flow of energy, the blocks dissolve more and more.

One woman who used this essence had an experience that showed this very clearly. Her fears had stopped her from driving a car for the past ten years. She had to do a great deal of business traveling and used only trains and taxis. After she had taken *Kamakura* for several days, she spontaneously rented a car and drove from Heidelberg to Hanover. Although she still was afraid, she no longer let the fear stop her from doing it.

This essence also supports people who hesitate in putting new abilities or new knowledge to use. Their argument is: "I can't do this right yet, I first have to learn more, I don't know enough." People who wait until they can do something perfectly will probably never start taking action because "practice makes perfect." All of our abilities and knowledge are useless if we don't put them to use.

New skills need to be applied so that a person truly masters them. In the same sense, children would never learn to ride bicycles if they only dared to ride when they could do it perfectly. The essence supports courage and stamina in such situations. Only when the things that we have learned are put to use can we judge what's still lacking, where the weak points and insecurities are. Without practical steps, a person stays stuck in his illusions about himself.

The *Kamakura* essence leads to powerful action, but in harmony with the needs of the body. When we go into activity and taking action too much without respecting boundaries, an exaggerated form of needless activity occurs and we damage ourselves and our surrounding world.

Someone who doesn't yet have any clear goals and fluctuates between a number of alternatives shouldn't use *Kamakura* before he has clarified his direction (for example, with *Orion*). In such cases, the energy starts to flow and a desire for action arises that tears us apart inwardly and lets us become restless because the energy can't be purposefully translated into action.

The situation is similar when dealing with work that hasn't yet been structured.

With the energy of *Kamakura* we come into a power that takes action. People who don't like getting up in the morning now wake up more quickly and become active. A joy in taking action arises. One woman told us that on the days that she uses the essence she achieves and accomplishes much more but has to watch out that she doesn't outdo herself and fall over her own feet. Another user expressed it like this: "I suddenly have so much energy that the day can hardly be long enough for me. And I take care of things with a speed and clarity that I hadn't experienced in myself up to now."

The Meditation

The meditation consists of three parts: in the first part, imagine that you are wandering through a greatly varied landscape. There are sections along your way in which you have to exert yourself, in which you climb mountains and swim in streams and lakes. And there are places where you stay for a while and rest. Here you simply enjoy lying in a meadow or on a beach. Take this path and observe when you take a break and when you continue on your way.

In the second part of the meditation, take the same path once again. However, before departing go into your center and experience the meditation from it. Go and don't go. Take action and sense your inner peace at the same time. This may be hard for you to do at the start.

In the third part, look at situations that you are facing in your own life. See what there is to do, see yourself taking action or not taking action, and follow the development of things with your inner eye. See how you apply all your strength, become conscious of the obstacles there are to overcome, and look at what happens when you simply let things happen.

When you carry out this meditation, you can take a leap in your everyday life, a leap to a level in which access to higher knowledge and your inner being, your center, opens up.

The Message

My friends, you have come to this earth in order to learn how to take action and how to let things happen. And this is not just a matter of chronological order. In some situations, it is also a matter of concurrence, that you do things and let things happen at the same time. This may appear to be a paradox to you at first, yet it is so only when you think in terms of duality, continuity, and in chronological order and not in the greater scope of things. In the greater scope of things, on the human level, you could very well take the steps that need to be taken and yet still be in the feeling that what you are setting into motion happens on its own. And whatever develops as a result, you let happen so that you are conscious in the moment that you do something that you are also passive and let it happen at the same time. This is the true harmony between the masculine and feminine sides of yourselves, the equilibrium.

Take the chronological order on the path that leaders you there. There are situations in which you take action and in which taking action is appropriate and successful. And there are situations and points in time when you do not take action but let things take their own course and let them happen. There are also points in time and situations where it is appropriate to let things happen and observe what happens. The difficulty for you is to recognize the points in time, in knowing when you should take action and when you should let things happen in order to achieve success. You will learn this by being in contact with your intuition, in contact with your Higher Self, and furthermore, in contact with the higher levels of consciousness. Then you will receive access to information that is important at the moment for you, for your decision, for your actions, and for your lack of actions.

When you consider all of this under the learning aspect, then what you do and what you don't do are both equally valid. Both have the same value since you learn no matter what decision you make and no matter what you do. And the more consciously you go through this process, the more consciously you will learn. And the more quickly you will learn. However, if you

175

strive for success and a pleasant life from your human perspective, then how you act is no longer of little consequence. Then it is appropriate for you to know when something should be done and what you should do. It is easiest for you to experience this when you are in contact with your higher levels of consciousness. On the basis of this sense of security, you can then apply all of your strength and energy in order to achieve what you want to achieve, take the steps that you want to take, and dissolve the blocks and learning steps that have not yet been completed. This transforms them.

I support you with my energy in doing this: in taking action at the right point in time, in consciously recognizing and transforming the blocks that occur, resulting in successful actions. This will also help you to be in contact with your own intuition and recognize the points in time to take action and the situations when you should not take action. You can then also see and dissolve the blocks and obstacles against not taking action so that you increasingly come into your center and then take action and exist on the basis of your composure and your center. My energy brings you into a state of taking calm action.

This does not mean that you should just sit there and do nothing or be lazy—this is a misunderstanding about the meaning of these words—but that you should take action from your own center in which you are centered, in which you are in your inner calmness and in your strength, and then you will act and be in a state of not acting at the same time, in a state of inner peace. With this I greet you.

No. 11—*Kuthumi*

Connecting with the Earth

The Effect of the Master Essence

The essence of *Kuthumi* opens us to the perception and the understanding of reality, supporting our sense of reality.

It connects with the earth energy and stimulates the flow of earth energy within the body. As a result, it gives us stability and promotes the connection between the subtle bodies and the physical bodies.

It helps us be more patient.

Kuthumi strengthens the perception of the earthly, subtle energy of places, stones, and living beings. It makes possible communication with other earthly beings like plants, gemstones, and fairies.

Associated with the chakras: Base chakra (heart chakra and crown chakra)
Color: Yellow
Tarot card: No. 6—The Lovers
Gemstone: Dendrite, amber, smoky quartz elastial
Oil application: Hairline on the forehead, forehead, third eye, foot chakras (soles of the feet), knees

A person who has balanced this aspect:
- "Stands with both feet on the ground."
- Is realistic; has a good intuition in relation to material things; also recognizes the correlations in economic situations.
- Perceives what projects will be successful.
- Has a good knowledge of human nature.
- Recognizes that matter is divine vibration.
- Has contact with the wisdom and knowledge of the earth; remembers rituals.
- Perceives the correlation between earthly circumstances (body, aura, and so forth).

A person who has not yet balanced this aspect:
- Isn't grounded.
- Gives the impression of a being from another world; isn't properly connected with the body; seems to not have any roots in the earth and will be uprooted by the next storm.
- Has problems with the reality of this earth.
- Loses sight of reality; evaluates events in an unrealistic way; doesn't have a feeling for how long processes take.
- Is very impatient.
- Is a "wanderer between the worlds"; reality isn't all that attractive for him, which is why he prefers to retreat to his castles in the sky; is dreamy and seldom completely in the present moment; is seldom receptive to earthly things like scientific findings, news, errands, which he feels to be unimportant.
- Tends towards illness, and often suffers from feelings of dizziness, weakness, and states of unreality without being physically sick; often has cold hands and feet; has little body consciousness and often bumps into things.

But also a person who:
- Is very materialistic and overly connected with earth, to whom the material aspects are excessively important.
- Sees the earth and the living beings of the earth as things to be exploited; uses the treasures of the earth in such as way as to destroy the earth and his own body in the long run.
- Rejects the existence of the subtle dimensions.

The difference between No. 11—Kuthumi, No. 7—Sanat Kumara, and No. 13—Seraphis Bey
on the theme of "connecting with the earth":

No. 11 opens the connection to the earth, letting us make friends with the earth.

No. 7 builds a bridge between heaven and earth, is an initial contact with the earth.

No. 13 leads into the middle of the material world and brings consciousness into matter.

Description

Kuthumi connects with the energy of the earth, with the body, and lets us become aware that we ourselves have chosen this planet and this body as our home. He opens our eyes for the idea that all being is connected and that living, divine energy flows in every part. Particularly in current times, many people have lost the connection with the earth. They live on this planet without really having a relationship to it. They use the treasures of the earth in a way that destroys the earth in the long run and also endangers their own bodies.

In addition to people who consider the earth to be a dead thing, there are others who don't like the energy of the earth. Particularly in the "esoteric movement," some people believe that the point is to turn away from earthly reality in order to transform earthly being and penetrate into higher realms of consciousness. They develop their higher realms of consciousness and neglect the contact with the earth. They have lost their grounding, which expresses itself in a one-sided view of the world and sometimes a body that is susceptible to illness as well. They virtually see just the subtle aspect and neglect the material reality. This is why people who believe in the esoteric teachings are often called dreamers and visionaries—or just plain out of touch with reality—by "normal people."

Kuthumi will become one of the most important masters for the development of humanity on the earth in the coming years. We are going into increasingly higher levels of consciousness and discovering more and more realms of subtle energy. When we develop ourselves in these areas, the connection with the earth is very important. If contact to the earth energy is broken, we also lose the connection with our body. A tree cannot grow without roots. The deeper its roots reach into the earth, the higher its crown can lift itself into the heavens. And those who have deep, stable roots can more easily withstand the storms of life.

The *Kuthumi* energy helps us to re-establish contact with the earth energy and our own body. It establishes the contact between the divine and the earthly aspect and therefore prepares the way for *Lady Nada*, who teaches us to accept and love our earthly body.

When we are connected with our earthly aspect, with our lower three chakras, the earth energy once again flows harmoniously through our body. The lower aura bodies connect more strongly with each other and give us grounding. They pass the earthly energy on to the other aura layers. We can more easily perceive the interaction between our body, the aura layers, the cosmic and earthy energy, and our surrounding world. This is because we influence our environment with our energy, and our environment influences us. We recognize what places support us and which ones are oppressive for us. We become more aware of the energies of the surrounding world and can therefore more easily recognize which plants, stones, gemstones, as well as people, are good for us.

However, the connection to the earth energy and its intensified flow through the body is not felt to be pleasant by everyone. As we started to work with the *Kuthumi* Essence, we had a feeling like lead weights on our feet, as if we were glued to the earth. Walking, dancing, and moving appeared to be more difficult and strenuous than before (we were also among the people who have a restricted flow of earth energy). After a while, we became accustomed to it and felt the earth energy to be quite pleasant. Our work became easier and we enjoyed it more than before.

A girlfriend had a similar experience. She had previously often suffered from feelings of dizziness and states of weakness because she hadn't been properly connected with her earthly body. Her entire appearance tended to be "angelic" and "unearthly," and she would have preferred not to be on the earth. When she began to take the *Kuthumi* Essence, she initially felt heavier. However, the states of weakness soon disappeared and she began to enjoy earthly life.

The strongest and quickest grounding can be achieved by applying the *Kuthumi* Oil to the foot chakras and hand chakras.

Another woman, who had too little connection with the earth, had difficulty breathing after she used the essence. She had made the decision for this essence on the basis of common sense since she knew that she had little grounding. However, her inner resistance against the earth energy was so strong that she blocked the energy flow through as little breathing as possible (deep breathing increases the flow of energy). It was easier for her to take the first step to grounding with Essence No. 7—*Sanat Ku-mara.*

Yet, *Kuthumi* not only helps to become more rooted here on the earth but also assists people who have a strong connection and relationship to the earth in opening up to the "spiritual side."

Every human being has a connection with the earth. We therefore potentially have the possibility of establishing contact with the earth's knowledge and wisdom. Not only people like Steiner and Paracelsus have been able to discover the secrets of the earth, take plants in their hands and say what healing powers they posses. Many people have the ability to sense energy from plants, gemstones, and so forth. They can perceive how plants, stones, and other things support the health of the body. *Kuthumi* helps us open these channels, making use of this knowledge and these abilities. We learn to "talk" to plants, and we can ask stones about their effect, their origin, and their history. It requires some practice in order to receive and comprehend this information. Sometimes memories of past knowledge, of rituals and techniques from past lives, are also revealed.

This energy also supports us in understanding scientific perspectives and more easily comprehending logical and scientific findings.

We can learn from nature that it takes time for things to be created. Nature knows the secret of the right point in time. Much of this already exists in thought form, but it needs time to be translated into the material form. The full-grown tree already existed in the seed of the tree—and yet it takes years until this tree becomes visible. The child in the womb already exists completely in the genes at the time of conception. However, it takes nine months until the body has formed itself. Both the seed and the growing child take the right steps at the right time. Matter is connected with time, and patience is required of us. *Kuthumi* teaches us to perceive and accept this fact. And to see the right point in time.

Kuthumi strengthens not only our eye for the visible world, but also opens the perception for subtle beings of the earth. Most adults are familiar with fairies, elves, gnomes, dwarfs, and water nymphs from fairy tales and shrug them off as "kids' stuff." However, these fairy tales originated at a time when there were more clairvoyant people who could perceive these forms of energy. These beings exist today as well. Sometimes small children tell us about everything that they see. If we look, we see nothing. Children often still possess the gift of perceiving these subtle beings. And we can also once again develop this ability. The *Kuthumi* energy helps us to do so, making it easier for us to communicate with these beings.

At the same time, the images of these human-like figures are in turn just a model for this subtle energy. Personification helps us to come into contact and communicate with these energies. The more familiar the picture, the easier it is for us to communicate with them.

The Meditation

Imagine that you are walking along a path. The path leads you through a meadow on a lovely sunny day or in the twilight. See the grasses and flowers, hear the insects and sounds of the meadow, and smell the fragrance.

Then perceive the beings that are in the meadow, that are with the flowers and grasses and the insects.

The path leads you into a forest. There you will also discover energy forms next to the trees and grasses. They support the growth of the plants and make sure that everything lives together in harmony. Perceive which tasks they have, and notice whether they establish contact with you and tell you of the earth and its wonders.

Then continue on your path until you reach a cave. Go into it and you will find a sea of crystals, colored stones in beautiful sparkling forms. There are also beings here. They live within the earth and guard the growth of the crystals. You can also establish contact with them, let them talk to you, and receive a message from them.

You path then leads you deep into the earth to the source of the earth energy. Experience this source and also notice whether there are beings at this place.

Then establish contact with the source of the earth energy in your own way. Let the energy flow through your body, perceive the condition and message of the earth, experience the source of earthly energy, and also sense your own source of earthly energy in your own body. Perceive what your energy flow is like, whether your foot chakras and hand chakras are open for the flow of earth energy, how the earth energy flows through your body, and whether there are places where it stagnates. You can heal these disorders at the source of the earth energy.

Then take your leave in the knowledge that you are connected with this source. Wherever you are on the earth, you are in contact with the earth's energy.

Now leave this cave and return to where you came from.

The Message

I support you with my energy so that you can once again open up to the interplay of the forces, so that you are once again in harmony with the vibration of the earth, so that you are once again connected with the energies of the earth in your thoughts, your feelings, and your being. This is how I support you so that this connection takes places and is intensified.

In addition, I support you so that you can perceive the beings of the earth, entities like elves and gnomes, subtle beings that guard the equilibrium of the earth and the harmony of plants, animals, and all being. This equilibrium takes place between the animal, plant, and mineral kingdoms.

Everything that takes place on the earth happens in harmony and has always been in harmony. Harmony doesn't mean a rigid fixity, but change and transformation—and this happens constantly. When this transformation occurs in an energetic equilibrium, something new is created. If it is productive, it nourishes the cycle of growth and decay. This is how it has always been.

However, when this equilibrium is wantonly destroyed by a disregard for the energetic processes, the point is then eventually reached where the balance of the earth can no longer be maintained and changes take place to such an extent that the cycle is disturbed. This happens when the beings of the earth or human beings lose contact with the earth, when they forget that a connection exists between not only the earth and the body but also between the consciousness of the earth and one's own consciousness. Interactions take place in this area as well. Human beings influence the powers of the earth, and the earth influences the people.

My energy opens up your perception for the laws of the earth, for harmony with the earth, for your path, and your interplay with the earth's energies. And I open up your heart so that the connection can happen in a loving way.

Learn to get back in contact and use the gifts of this earth in a way that benefits both the earth and humanity. Perceive where the earthly portion of your existence originated.

The beings and the energy of the earth that support this process are with me so that the human beings can once again establish contact with this earth, with the planet that they have chosen as their homeland and home for a certain period of time.

Let yourselves once again be touched by the entities of the earth and the earth's energy. Make friends, and you will become various forms of support for your being and your life.

No. 12—*Lady Nada*

Being Accepted and Enjoying Life

The Effect of the Master Essence

The essence of *Lady Nada* makes emotional healing possible—
it heals the feeling of having a deficit in terms of love.   At the
same time, it supports us in accepting our body.

It makes us aware of what we really want and what nourishes
us—which people, relationships, places, food, and environments
are good for us.

It challenges us to see what we lack for our well-being and
how we hinder ourselves in our feeling of wellness.

The essence intensifies the sensory perceptions—of music,
fragrances, and experiences of nature.

It strengthens the connection to the "inner healer" and makes
to possible for us to integrate feminine qualities and the feminine
principle.

Associated with the chakras: Heart chakra (sacral chakra)
Color: Pink
Tarot card: No. 2—The High Priestess
Gemstone: Pink tourmaline, rose quartz
Oil application: Back and front of the chest area, stomach area,
    parts of the body that aren't loved, as well as the outside of
    the ankle.

A person who has balanced this aspect:
- Accepts himself like he is, unconditionally.
- Feels well, accepted, and has a sense of security in his body
  and his surroundings.
- Takes care of his body and pays attention to its needs—to the
  proper amount of food, sleep, and exercise.
- Recognizes his true needs; fulfills his desires without hamper-
  ing others in the process.

A person who has not yet balanced this aspect:
- Rejects himself and his body.
- Has lost contact with the body; doesn't have a feeling for his body.
- Doesn't find himself attractive; believes his body is ugly and doesn't like to look at himself in the mirror, which results in insecure behavior.
- Constantly needs approval and recognition from the outside, but can't ever get enough of it.
- Has many wishes, but their fulfillment isn't truly satisfying.
- Doesn't act in accordance with his needs, although he knows what they are; doesn't pay attention to his body and take proper care of it; eats too much; sleeps too much or too little; gets too little exercise.
- Lives a sexuality that doesn't fulfill him and doesn't make him happy; often no longer enjoys sexuality and is dissatisfied.
- Is self-destructive; also encounters others in a self-destructive manner.

But also a person who:
- Overemphasizes physical pleasures.

The difference between No. 12—Lady Nada and No. 2—Lao Tse on the theme of "condemnation and nonacceptance":

No. 12 transforms by accepting one's own value.
No. 2   transforms by ending the condemnation.

Description

Lady Nada helps us to accept ourselves with our light and shadow aspects. We live more tolerance towards ourselves and unconditionally say "yes" to ourselves, to our body, and to our life. Just as Christ teaches unconditional love as a principle, Lady Nada shows us this unconditional love for ourselves and our body. This means that we should pay attention to the body's needs, respect the body, look at its desires, recognize the true wishes and needs, and then act accordingly. We notice the moments when we overlook our needs and which parts of our own body we don't like.

We recognize our shadow sides, learning to accept and integrate them. At the moment in which we truly succeed in accepting them, they will transform themselves. They no longer hide in the shadows but are brought into the light of consciousness— they become illuminated. We learn to say: "I am a human being and confront the light and shadow aspects through which I grow. I go my way partly consciously and partly unconsciously, and I love myself with my strengths and weaknesses."

Some people fear that the unloved sides will get stuck and cemented to them if they stop fighting and start accepting them. But this isn't the case. Change is the result of true acceptance. Things naturally don't work out if we accept the shadow aspects solely for the purpose of changing them. As long as we treat them in this way, we haven't really said "yes" to these aspects.

There have been a variety of experiences with the *Lady Nada* essence. Some people immediately feel themselves to be accepted. They feel well, enveloped, and secure.

After a strenuous drive of four hours, one woman who used it felt very good and also looked at ease and relaxed, although she would normally have been completely exhausted.

"I could sing the whole day. Everyone should use the *Lady Nada* energy. It brings you into the most wonderful state that I've experienced," said one of the other women who used it. She therefore gave her best friend a *Lady-Nada* Energy Ball. However, at the start the girlfriend didn't do well with it at all. She became aware of how much she condemned herself. She believed that nothing she did was good enough. She started to feel ugly and unattractive, although she is a good-looking woman. For a time, she didn't even like looking at herself in the mirror. Although she realized that her reaction had nothing to do with reality—she noticed that men still gazed at her in admiration— she suffered from her own condemnation.

This woman first had to become aware of her inner resistance against "being accepted." She remembered how she had an upbringing that was hostile to the body and that she had suppressed her needs for many years. Only after she recognized her pattern of behavior and became conscious of her wishes and needs did she start to like the energy of *Lady Nada*.

Another attractive, slender woman took the *Lady Nada* Essence during her vacation on the beach. During the first days she only noticed "fat, limping, and ugly people" and said to herself time and again: "That's what I look like too." However, at the same time she could laugh about herself. After several days, she was able to recognize and accept her own beauty.

These experiences show how different people react to the Master Essences.

I also saw my wounds in relation to "being accepted" during the time with *Lady Nada*. For example, I wanted to give an acquaintance a piece of clothing that had become too wide for me. She didn't like it and didn't take it—I could have cried and felt rejected, although I could very well see that my reaction had nothing to do with what had happened. During this time, I interpreted many occurences as rejection until I began to look at this emotion and accepted the feeling of "being rejected." Afterwards, I got along very well with this essence.

As person who can accept himself is more easily able to accept others. He no longer projects his shadow sides to the outside, and he no longer encounters them in the form of other people who reflect his suppressed behavior to him. He no longer has to constantly be aggravated about other people who do the things that he himself suppresses and doesn't want to see.

Someone who works with the *Lady Nada* Essence will also see his own blocks against "having a good time" if he believes he isn't allowed to enjoy life and doesn't deserve wealth, happiness, and abundance. He discovers when he rejects and suppresses his joy in life and the pleasures of the senses, when restrictive beliefs take effect like: "That isn't good for you," "That's too much of a good thing," "That's not proper," "Don't count your chickens before they hatch," and "Pride goes before a fall." He becomes clear about what mechanisms develop that prevent him from enjoying a complete state of happiness.

Someone who has lived in a way that restricts joy for a longer period of time finds his thoughts circling increasingly around his deficits. When the arising deficit, the "inner hunger" is balanced through pleasant and nourishing experiences, feelings, and occurences, a state of "being fulfilled" is achieved. However, a person thinks constantly about eating as long as he is hungry. Then it's almost impossible to think about anything else. On the other hand, after a tasty feast there are no more thoughts about eating. Then it is easy to concentrate on something else.

Several days after using the essence, a woman who was overweight and constantly suffered from feelings of hunger had the image of a yellow ball approaching her and filling her solar plexus chakra. The feelings of hunger subsided thereafter.

The energy of *Lady Nada* particularly heals the emotional body in this way. The love deficit is filled and healed. More self-confidence is the result.

Lady Nada teaches us to recognize and enjoy the pleasant things in life. She lets us experience music in a new way, both music created by human beings and the music of nature. Fragrances and touch can be perceived in a more intense way as a result.

If we live in harmony with the body, we will receive access to its wisdom. The body then shows us very clearly what is good for it, what nourishes it, which people give us support and who costs us our strength. We pay attention to nutritious food, nurturing people, and nourishing relationships.

The contact with the "inner healer," the part that knows what it wants, what we are lacking, and how we can become whole again, is intensified. It is then possible to receive advice from it. You can support it with the following method:

Relax and establish contact with your body. In your thoughts, wander through your body and thank the individual parts and organs for their work. Become aware of the work that the respective body part does for you. If you can, also thank the sick parts of the body since these just want to draw your attention to what you need in order to become whole and complete and live a fulfilled life. Afterwards, direct your consciousness to the part of the body that is sick and ask it what it wants to say to you and what you can do in order to become healthy again. Ask the body part or your inner healer to support you in becoming healthy.

At the start, some people have a hard time establishing contact and understanding the body's message. However, if this exercise is repeated, the contact becomes easier with time and the information can be better understood.

The essence of *Lady Nada* also includes the confrontation with the theme of sexuality and the joys of sexuality. It lets us ask ourselves if we are satisfied with our sexuality and what we desire. The sexual energy in particular is a potential for joy in life and for liveliness. When we open ourselves for the fulfillment of our needs, this is also part of it. There are many wounds, tabus, and unpleasant experiences regarding this in our society. And it is often difficult to get help because the affected people don't have the courage to address this topic.

If sexuality is lived in a fulfilling way, a great reservoir of energy opens up. This has a healing effect on our life, our body, and our relationships.

The essence promotes the development of the feminine principle and feminine qualities. Among these are: enjoying life, feeling yourself to be accepted, letting yourself be showered with life's gifts and accepting them, intuitive perception, feeling, premonition, the ability to love, the relationship to nature and to the deeper areas of the psyche, dreams and visions, composure, and cheerfulness.

Every human being has a masculine and a feminine side within, and the goal is to develop and use both aspects in our life. If we neglect one part, it will often express itself in a negative way. An example of this is when the unlived feminine quality of "feeling" expresses itself as moodiness and irritability.

The Meditation

Do a meditation of the senses. Either in your thoughts or with your feet, walk through a forest or a field with flowers and look at the colors, listen to the music of nature, smell the fragrance, and pay attention to your feelings. Or listen to music and look at colors and pictures or perceive fragrances and feelings together with the music.

In closing, imagine that you are wrapped up in a warm, pink coat, perhaps inside a fur or in rose petals that are soft and cuddly.

If you want to take a further step, you can see yourself sitting in the universe wrapped in flower petals with a feeling of wellness and acceptance.

The Message

I greet you, you happy beings who possess a body.

Accept my greeting and learn to enjoy the possibilities concealed in this body, to experience the joys of the earth, to savour them and taste the richness of life. See the beauty that surrounds you, smell the fragrances that make life pleasant for you, warm your souls, and please your hearts. Taste the sumptuous foods and things that are here on this earth. Listen to the music of nature and the music created by human beings. Blossom along with it. And also enjoy your sense of touch: touch nature, a tree, a bush, a stone. Hold your hand in water and feel how the water flows. Experience this enjoyment, feel the stone that lies in the bed of a stream. See how it feels to touch the grass and the fur of cats and dogs. Enjoy the experiences of the senses, which are not possible without this body.

Also enjoy your bodies by bathing, by massaging each other and letting yourselves be massaged, by wrapping yourselves in lovely materials and letting a fragrance waft in the air. Experience touch and the play of energies in your sexuality. Enjoy this life.

Let your body feel good in this way, accept it and pay attention to its needs like being massaged, oiled, exercised, accepted, touched, and enveloped in lovely fragrances and clothing. Fulfill these needs and it will be much easier for you to create the things that you now consider to be great. In this way, it will be natural for you to have things go well. This theme is the first step to overcoming the material world, so to speak, by letting yourselves feel good in this material world. When all the needs have been fulfilled there, then you can grow into the divine as well, without losing the material world, without having to push it away. You will extend yourselves and unite the material and the divine.

Some of you will certainly reply that there is more than just the lovely aspects of this earth and that unlovely things like hate, stench, and noise exist on this earth as well. You will naturally have an increased perception of this as well because you live in the world of duality. And you can no longer recognize the beauty without the things that are ugly, you cannot perceive the harmony in music without dissonant music, you cannot enjoy the stillness without having experienced the noise. So you will naturally also be very conscious of the opposite side in the process. Take a look at it.

And you can choose. You can choose whether you go into the pleasure or into the other side. It is part of your human life to become familiar with both sides and also experience them in part. You will more easily accept this, and you have the free choice of whether you want to look at the beautiful things or the ugly. You can choose whether you enjoy the stillness of the forest and the music of nature as often as possible or wander through the noise of your streets.

You will say that there are obligations like going shopping, working, and so forth.

And you are right.

Yet, you can perceive the beautiful aspects in all things and support yourselves in also perceiving the beauty. Enjoy what there is to enjoy at this moment. At the same time, see that there are also other aspects and, if you want, experience both of them.

Since both things are there are the same time, you have the opportunity of going beyond them into something new, something that develops. If many people can take this step, much will change on this earth.

And so I challenge you time and again to enjoy life and completely accept yourselves!

No. 13—*Seraphis Bey*

The Earthly Power

The Effect of the Master Essence

This essence intensifies and harmonizes the energy flow of the first chakra.

It lets us breath deeper, which strengthens and improves the energy balance. The essence gets energy flowing and makes it effective. It brings energy from the physical body into the energy body and stimulates movement. It opens up the body's power reserves, whereby the effect is intensified by sports, dancing, and physical exercise.

The essence brings consciousness into matter.

It helps overly rational people get into contact with their body and perceive it. It strengthens the connection between the 3rd and 4th chakras, which thereby intensifies the connection between the lower three aura layers and the spiritual aura body.

The essence cleanses earthly matter. It can therefore be used for cleansing the aura, rooms, and gemstones.

It helps us go into the material world in meditation, experiencing and understanding it from the inside.

Seraphis Bey *supports shamanic work.*

Associated with the chakras: Base chakra (sacral chakra and throat chakra)
Color: White
Tarot card: No. 15—The Devil
Gemstone: Red garnet, black tourmaline
Oil application: Medulla (back of head, at upper end of spinal column), on the center line of the abdomen between pubic hair and navel, and on the back at the same level (apply from bottom to top); in addition: inward side of knee

A person who has balanced this aspect:

- Accepts his animalistic power and uses it; integrates his strength; has perceived that the animalistic side isn't crude and violent and knows the difference between strength and violence.
- Feels himself to be powerful; has a healthy, strengthened body.
- Has a relationship to the material world; likes to work with and form matter.
- Also lives pleasure in sexuality.
- Is fascinated by the earthly world, wants to comprehend and experience it.
- Is aware of his own earthly roots and knows how he can use them.
- Likes to work with physical force.

A person who has not yet balanced this aspect:

- Has little life energy; has problems with bones and teeth.
- Condemns strength and powerful people as being coarse and without feelings; experiences the animalistic energy and aspect of life as coarse and destructive; is afraid of and rejects it.
- Rejects a powerful body and is usually quite weak in appearance.
- Is overly rational and thinks constantly; has little relationship to his body and his feelings.
- Is nervous and jumpy.
- Has problems experiencing the feeling of love; love remains intellectual.

But also a person who:

- Lives in a very physically oriented and hedonistic way.
- Glorifies physical strength.

The difference between No. 13—Seraphis Bey and No. 11—Kuthumi on the theme of "connecting with the earth":

No. 13 Seraphis Bey brings us into the middle of the material world, allows us to understand (goes into the depths), connects with our own earthly roots, opens up the first chakra.

No. 11 Kuthumi connects with the energy of the earth, with the entity of earthly forms of being (goes into the breadth), opens up the foot chakras for the flow of earth energy.

Description

Seraphis Bey is the creator in the material world. He brings consciousness into matter, makes us aware of what the material world is and how it is possible to create in earthly matter. He teaches us the creator quality in the earthly realm.

Along with *Sanat Kumara* and *Kuthumi*, *Seraphis Bey* also brings us into the material world, into the body. Of these three, he is the master who guides us deep into the material world, who brings consciousness and our state of consciousness into our earthly aspect and lets us understand the matter. In meditations I have experienced his energy as light roots. My roots went deep into the earth and were made of light, while my consciousness wandered deep into the earth, into matter. *Seraphis Bey* allows us to perceive, accept, and love earthly existence. This applies to both the earthly, animalistic aspect of our being, as well as the "world outside."

Some people condemn the animalistic side of their being as coarse, insensitive, inhuman, unconscious, and thereby cut themselves off from its life-giving strength. They condemn the powerful energy of survival that makes sure we don't lose ourselves in the mental spiritual realms but take care of our body, that lets us look for food when we are hungry, that lets us seek warmth when we are freezing, that gives us sexual desire so that we reproduce ourselves.

When we condemn all of this, we constrict the flow of earthly life energy. This not only leads to a weakening of the body but also prevents the step into unity since we can only be one when we accept the earthly aspect. This can't happen when we condemn or limit it.

How should we develop ourselves in a spiritual sense when the body is too weak? When we don't really take care of the body, when we are weak and sick, we don't have enough energy available for our spiritual growth. When we continue to develop ourselves spiritually, the subtle portions of our body begin to vibrate at a higher frequency. But when our connection to the body isn't strong enough in this case, there is danger of it breaking off. When our interest and our spiritual cooperation with the body diminishes, the body no longer receives enough energy and then becomes ill. When we lose the contact and the love of our body or reject earthly existence, we often become stuck in destructive addictions or use the body like a tool. We become unfeeling towards ourselves and material things.

Seraphis Bey leads us to our own earthly power and to the animalistic legacy within us. He brings light to these aspects and supports us in consciously accepting them. While *Kuthumi* opens the connection to the earth and the foot chakras, *Seraphis Bey* cleanses our first chakra and lets its energy flow more intensely through us.

People who emphasize the physical aspects too much or have a self-destructive approach to their body (through addictions, for example) should start with the essence of *Kuthumi* and then use the *Seraphis Bey* Essence. They will open themselves for the energy of the earth through *Kuthumi* and strengthen the energy flow within the body. They make friends with the body and the earth. As a result, *Seraphis Bey* brings consciousness into the material world.

To bring light into matter also means cleansing matter and once again allowing it to become a pure vibration. The essence can therefore be applied for the cleansing of all material things, such as for the cleansing of your own body from oppressive energies and the cleansing of rooms, auras, gemstones, places, and plants.

In case you already use rituals for cleansing purposes, you can include the essence of *Seraphis Bey* in them. If you haven't used any type of ritual up to now, here is a suggestion: Put some oil or tincture in the palm of your hand and spread around the energy in your aura by moving your hands, with the palms turned towards your body, from the top to the bottom through your aura. Then pause for a moment while the vibration is distributed within your aura and streams to the outside through the palms of your hands. You can then let the energy flow into the objects that you want to cleanse. For example, put gemstones in your hand and let them by permeated by the energy. You can fill rooms with light from your hands. In closing, give thanks for the support and take your leave of the master energy.

You can also create your own cleansing rituals.

The *Seraphis Bey* Essence supports people who do therapeutic work on the body (massage therapists, body workers, healing practitioners, and so forth) to go into matter with their consciousness and understand the correlations. Information about all other forms of material being become accessible in the same way, such as information from stones, gemstones, and trees. In contrast to *Kuthumi*, we receive information about the material aspect such as structure, contents, and effects from *Seraphis Bey*.

The Meditation

Let the consciousness in your body wander slowly into a chakra.

From there, slide down to the pelvic floor with your consciousness in a spiral form, as if you were in a spiral made of white light. When you have reached the pelvic floor, perceive what your first chakra is like. What color is it and what shape does it have? From what material does it appear to be made of—is it soft or hard? Where are dark spots and where is it light? How far does it extend and how does it feel? Does it have a sound, a melody, or fragrance? If it were a plant, what plant would it be? If it were an animal, what animal would it be?

Then start to vibrate around the core in a spiral pattern. Stretch the spiral further and further, as far as you can go. It may be that you can sometimes go very far, but at other times you already have enough after a few inches.

Observe this process. Observe the images and thoughts that come up.

The Message

I greet you, my friends, and accompany you on the earth. I support you in going deep down into the first chakra, deep down into your earthly, animalistic power. I support you in accepting it and transforming it. The dark aspects and shadows of earthly existence will certainly also come into consciousness when you do this. So confront the animalistic aspects of yourselves, and you will evaluate many things to be positive and many things to be negative. Here it should also be said that there is neither positive nor negative—it is as it is.

So immerse yourselves in your earthly power, in your earthly consciousness, and live it.

You cannot have much of an effect here on the earth, and also will not take any greater spiritual steps, if you are not connected with the first chakra and if it does not vibrate in harmony with all the other chakras. Only when it does can you blossom and develop yourselves equally on all levels of your existence. This is why the development of the first chakra—which is often constricted, imbalanced, or blocked in "spiritual" people—is an important task. It is absolutely necessary for your spiritual growth to include grounding and the first chakra so that you perceive what it means to be here on the earth, to live with the earth, to live with your strength and so that you learn how you can use your animalistic power for yourselves and your success without hurting others. You will therefore go through this process, which will bring some things to light that you haven't yet seen.

Learn to integrate this power into yourselves. Then you can truly work in the material world and cause something to happen. You attain access to the laws of the material world, and you can shape it. Not only will you shape your own narrow material world, but you will shape more. All aspects of material existence are a part of the material world.

My color ray is white, and I cleanse you with it. I bring the light of consciousness deep into your roots, into your origins. I bring light and cleanse the shadow sides, of which you will then become aware. So don't be frightened. Look at them and let them be transformed by perceiving and accepting them.

No. 14—*Victory*

Growth

The Effect of the Master Essence

The *Victory* Master Essence stabilizes and enlarges the aura and supports the exchange within the aura. The result is a better connection and communication between the layers.

It removes the blocks between the chakras, between the aura bodies, between the unconscious mind, the Higher Self, and the waking consciousness, harmonizing the energy systems with each other. These attune themselves to each other and information is exchanged at a quicker pace.

It strengthens the connection of body, mind, and soul.

The effect of the essence is strongest at places that have the most intensive blocks and disorders. It therefore helps in working out the pending themes and bringing them to consciousness.

The essence supports every type of energetic body work.

It can be particularly recommended for integration and harmonization after and before the beginning of a new task or phase in life, as well as for "aura hygiene."

A person who intuitively chooses *Victory* is possibly standing at threshold of something new in life.

Associated with the chakras: All
Color: White with all the colors like an opal
Tarot card: No. 14—Temperance (Art)
Gemstone: Tourmaline quartz
Oil application: Cervical vertebra (the one that sticks out the most in the neck area); as well as the spinal column, applied from bottom to top.

A person who has balanced this aspect:
• Has a harmonious flow of energy in the body; his aura is stable and whole.

- Is in harmony with himself and with the higher conscious-ness, receiving self-assurance and composure as a result.
- Recognizes where he stands and what steps come next.
- Lives in joyful confidence; learning steps are accepted.

A person who has not yet balanced this aspect:
- Doesn't recognize where he is blocked.
- Is unclear about things and doesn't have the energy to do something in order to change this condition.
- Doesn't have a harmony between the energy bodies; for ex-ample, thought and feeling deviate strongly from each other.
- Has a weak and defective aura and easily loses energy to others and the surrounding world; others can easily draw en-ergy from him.

Description

The *Victory* energy harmonizes the energy flow within the entire energy system. It breaks down blocks and balances the flow of information between the body and the subtle layers, within the chakras, the aura bodies, and between the chakras and the aura bodies. As a result, the aura is stabilized and enlarged. The connection and communication between the aura layers is in-tensified and information exchanged more quickly. The chakras attune themselves to each other and vibrate in harmonious to-getherness.

The permeability between waking consciousness, the uncon-scious mind, and the Higher Self is also increased. The access to our own abilities, to stored knowledge, to potential and intui-tion—in short, to everything that is needed at the moment—be-comes more easily possible. The connection of the body, mind, and soul is strengthened.

In order to achieve a stronger connection of the chakras with each other, it is recommended that you apply the essence to the center line of the body. When doing this, it is important to spread the essence from the bottom to the top, meaning from the 1st to the 7th chakra.

When working with this energy, the greatest effects will occur where the strongest blocks and disorders are. If you know with which theme or chakra you have a problem, you can specifically use the essence there. It helps us in working through themes, looking at our own resistance, and recognizing the deeper-lying cause.

If there are a great many disorders in the energy system or you can't decide on one theme or Master Essence, the application of the *Victory* energy clarifies the theme that we could best work on at the moment. We comprehend the pending learning steps and how the themes are related to each other.

We can take inventory with *Victory*. And we can recognize what is stopping us from being connected with the divine source. Writing down what we are concerned with—what apprehensions, fears, and worries occur during the course of the day—supports this perception.

The *Victory* Essence can be easily combined with all the other Master Essences. It lets us look at things more clearly, seeing and recognizing our own standpoint, desires, and goals. After each step of development, it integrates what has been attained into the energy system and brings the individual portions into harmony.

People who want to achieve a clear perspective of the pending learning steps are supported by this energy. And it makes it easier to go into new experiences and lose the fear of something new.

Victory is the transition of the series "living the immortal part in the earthly world" to the section "integration within the self." It is the transition into a new quality, the breakthrough in order to combine all levels of existence with each other. When someone intuitively selects *Victory*, this may mean that he is also standing on the threshold to something new in his life. Then the energy encourages him to joyfully try out new things.

The work with this energy strengthens a person's self-confidence and trust in his own abilities, above all in situations of change. It's like starting the next class after successful completing the last one at school. We know that new tasks and new material are waiting to be learned. However, on the basis of experience we also know that exactly the same thing was true in the previous class and we mastered it. We know that the material to be learned progresses slowly, that we learn in small steps and then develop a joyful, relaxed confidence about the new things.

One woman who used this essence had a position at a company that was far below her level of qualification. However, she no longer thought that she was capable anymore and hadn't even looked for another job. After she worked with the *Victory* Essence, she was offered a position appropriate to her qualifications at her present company—and accepted it. Previously, she would have rejected it because of her feelings of insecurity.

The Meditation

After relaxing, imagine how the first chakra becomes filled with light. Perceive what color it has. It may be white, red, or any other color. Let the color simply come. Each color that you perceive is right. In case no color comes at all, then imagine white light or let a feeling of purity, expansiveness, and openness flow into it.

Let the light expand, rotating in the form of a spiral throughout your entire body from your feet to your head. And then let it continue to grow through all the layers of the aura. While the light is expanding, perceive how it hits against dark blocks, limitations, and constrictions—and transforms them. Perhaps images arise, perhaps you see situations or become aware of something for the first time. You see wishes that haven't yet been fulfilled and disappointments that you carry with you. Let them be transformed in the white light. And if there are things that are not yet ready to be transformed, then accept them as they are. They still serve a function and support you on the path in their own way.

Work intensively with the first chakra, and do this until you feel good about its condition. Then go further into the second and repeat this process up to the sixth chakra. The seventh chakra leads you to the divine source, into the center of your being.

When you have reached the seventh chakra, use the meditation of the divine source, as described under Saint Germain, for a while. Be in divinity, see the light around yourself, and see how the light emanates from you and radiates. See how it illuminates your surroundings and how everything that you need comes to you in this divinity. This meditation supports the process and is a strong purification. You can go through this process time and again. It cleanses and harmonizes.

At the beginning of the work with the *Victory* energy, it is recommended that you do this meditation in sections, working with the first chakra for a while. When this has been cleansed, then continue with the first and second. The first chakra needs less time when this is repeated.

The Message

The path into the light leads over stones that you have placed in your way. So you then climb up and down in order to free yourselves from the entanglements that you have created for yourselves in order to have your experiences and expand your consciousness. You take this path, which is sometimes difficult and arduous for you on the earthly and human level. Sometimes it is full of suffering, fear, and mistrust, and sometimes it is full of light, happiness, and joy. However, the entire path is full of light on your higher levels of consciousness. You are welcome and welcome this path yourself. It is your growth, and you confront all the aspects of your existence on the earth in your growth. So wander through your chakras. When you have finished going through them once, start again at the first chakra. At some time in your earthly existence it will be time to make the decision of ending this arduous path into the darkness. Then you will turn around and go into the light. Then you will begin to heal your wounds, transform the entanglements and burdens, clarify the experiences, and come to your selves.

My energy leads you through this path. It supports you at the places where you have cleansed yourselves and everything comes back into harmony and attunement in order to take the next step. All the chakras and all of your energy bodies become filled with light. Light floods through you.

No. 15—*Saint Germain*

Freedom

The Effect of the Master Essence

This essence makes us aware of our own beliefs and patterns of behavior, frees us from "stickiness" in the emotional and mental bodies and from karma, leading us to inner freedom. This makes it possible for us to see situations from other perspectives and be free to choose what we do and how we react.

It makes it possible for us to receive an impression of what it means to be in one's own divinity.

Associated with the chakras: Throat chakra (forehead chakra)
Color: Violet
Tarot card: No. 18—The Moon
Gemstone: Amethyst, amethyst-quartz rosette, charoite
Oil application: Forehead chakra, throat, particular in the area of the larynx; 7th cervical vertebra

A person who has balanced this aspect:
- Lives in a state of "inner freedom"; sees the possibilities for taking action and is free to make decisions.
- Is familiar with his roles and masks and can freely decide which ones to put aside or when to use them.
- Enjoys the liveliness of life; experiences intensively without becoming caught up in it.
- Has a differentiated way of looking at things, can look at situations from many perspectives and recognizes many aspects.
- Enjoys verbal expression.
- Confronts the theme of "joy and suffering"; sees the suffering of this world and recognizes the deeper significance and correlations without suffering along with it.
- Can smile in amusement at suffering and drama and the game of life without laughing at it; feels empathy.
- Has freed himself from karmic entanglements.

A person who has not yet balanced this aspect:
- Is stuck in the suffering and pain of life; attracts suffering over and over again in his life.
- Feels himself to be restricted by obligations and constraints.
- Is caught in oppressive patterns of thinking and feeling.
- Feels himself to be in conflict between the various inner beliefs and ideas.

But also a person who:
- Doesn't takes anything seriously; sees everything as a game, but doesn't recognize the learning task it contains.
- Plays the cheerful clown who always laughs and makes others laugh for the outside world but is deeply sad and unfulfilled within.

The difference between No. 15—Saint Germain and No. 1—Maha Chohan on the theme of "entanglements":

No. 15 makes us aware of our own inner beliefs, patterns of behavior, and entanglements. As a result, we are no longer inwardly imprisoned and can make a free choice.

No. 1 leads out of the entanglement because we take a step back and get a more detached view of things.

Description

The theme of *St. Germain* is freedom—freedom from old entanglements, from inner limitations, old patterns, masks, and constraints'. This means freedom from everything that stops us from living our "being." He helps us recognize karmic patterns and see what holds us prisoner in the unconscious mind. He frees us through transformation and the process of becoming conscious.

When I ran into a girlfriend after not seeing her for some time, she had separated six months before from a man with whom she had lived for several months. It hadn't been possible for her to separate from him, even though the situation with him had increasingly deteriorated for her. This man had now returned to her town. When she saw him, she immediately collapsed inwardly and became small and powerless. I gave her *St. Germain*, and she applied the oil to her third eye and throat repeatedly during the day. That very same evening, she encountered the man at a party. And now she could suddenly remain in her power and self-confidence. She went to him and greeted him, was able to give him a hug, and then soon took her leave of him again. There was no longer a connection between them.

The essence frees us from stickiness in the emotional and mental aura bodies. This makes it possible to look at things in a different way and with another perspective. A deep understanding becomes possible. We observe our patterns of behavior, recognize the beliefs and concepts behind them, and free ourselves of rigid structures, old patterns, and ways of behaving in which we have become stuck. We achieve freedom through consciousness, through a recognition of the correlations between our own situation and the role we play.

We live "self-evidently," from the understanding of the self. As a result, we integrate divine and earthly being and can more easily take the steps on the earth. The path of liberation leads to "consciousness of the self."

St. Germain shows us what it means to be free of karmic and earthly entanglements.

This makes life a pleasure—it prickles like champagne. Then we can also look at drama and suffering from another perspective. We succeed in both smiling about this game and being empathetic towards it at the same time. And we succeed in getting an impression of what it means to live out of our own divine being.

A feeling of inner conflict may arise at first when you use this essence. You may be pulled back and forth between the various spiritualized beliefs, concepts, and experiences. These become conscious, and now you are free to choose in accordance with the inner concepts and beliefs you want to live. And you are free change this around again at any time.

One woman who used this essence was involved in developing her own livelihood. She became aware of all the inner phrases related to the theme of "being a self-employed entrepreneur." She felt herself torn back and forth between self-assurance and the oppressive maxims of failure, between the ones that said to her: "You've succeeded at everything that you started up to now" and "you've already seen so many other people fail—why should things go better for you?—You have much too little experience for this work." This made it more clear to her why she had met with so many difficulties up to now. After she had seen this and dissolved the oppressive maxims, she took the subsequent steps more courageously and freely.

One man who used this essence reported: after he had started with the *St. Germain* Essence, he received a large job assignment. This was actually a reason to be happy, but he felt oppressed. When he suddenly became aware of this, he took a closer look at things and noticed his fears and disappointment. He realized that for him success was connected with the idea of: "now things are ending, this will be my ruin." This idea was completely nonsensical, but that's how it was. It became clear to him that he had already had this pattern for years. Whenever a big opportunity for success came up, he became afraid, felt bad, and had the idea that "things are going to end now." And this sentence also came up for him: "if you climb up high, you can fall far." This had always held him back when his success became "too big." He had never been aware of this before. Now it was suddenly quite clear to him, triggered by the assignment, and he found it easy to transform the old thought pattern.

St. Germain is also suitable for people who brood too much, who rack their brains, who worry a great deal because they just see the suffering of this world and are crushed by it. These people attract hardship and suffering time and again.

This doesn't mean that we should deny and ignore pain and suffering, just as little as we should reject joy, desire, or happiness. Every exclusion of one pole makes the state of being incomplete even greater. Two opposite poles always belong to our duality. The world consists of light and shadow, of suffering and joy. Both qualities are in this world and we can find two sides to every part of it. If we just notice the suffering, then we see just half of the truth. If we just notice the joy, then we see just half of the truth. Only when we observe both the light and shadow aspects do we see everything. So the essence also makes it possible to see the interplay of light and shadow, of day and night within ourselves.

There are a great variety of concepts behind the definition of "freedom." *St. Germain* told us what he understands to be freedom during a channeling session, the text of which is included here:

"The theme about which I will speak today is the theme of freedom and what being free means to me.

To be free doesn't mean withdrawing from all the structures and obligations, being on a lonely island or alone in the mountains. You can be just as unfree there as you can be free in structures and restrictions. It is a misunderstanding found in your world. You human beings create so much pressure and burdens for yourselves that you mistake "being free" with the state of being without burdens. Sometimes you understand for a brief moment that freedom is found within you and sense how it is to feel yourselves free.

However, you generally mistake it for the abolishment of all burdens and obligations. To be in divinity is freedom. Freedom means being able to choose on your own what you do and what you do not do. Freedom means doing everything that you want in an inner state of peace, as a foregone conclusion. Freedom means not letting yourself be restricted, not letting yourself be burdened by the things that you do, and also not becoming addicted to the pattern of always "having to do" something. You know quite precisely that there is nothing that you have to do. But this "doing nothing" naturally has its own consequences. And because you do not want to bear these consequences, you decide to do something.

It is not true that someone else can make the decisions affecting you and that the structures can force you to do things. It is ultimately a question of your own will, and you always make the decision. You also decide when to set your own will aside, and when you live will not your own will but someone else's will. This is also ultimately your decision.

The path of achieving freedom is the path of standing up for yourself, of assuming responsibility, and seeing that everything that you do arises of your own will and freedom to make decisions. And also to see and feel what power and strength you achieve as a result, and how you can go with the flow and are able to make a decision at any moment. This is a step towards freedom.

The next step is freedom in your thoughts so that you are surrounded by light. Then you will radiate to the outside world and have the light within you that fills and enlightens you. You will live your own light and this light will fill you so much that all thoughts, beliefs, and patterns drop away.

You are in the stream of light and live out of this light. You live and go your own way. Do what you want to do on the basis of inner peace and inspiration, being completely in the moment and completely present. Freedom is enlightenment, being one, and being in harmony. And freedom means being in accord, using the energy of the moment, and taking your own steps. It means using the coldness of the environment in order to experience your own warmth, using the sun and sunny days in order to sense and nourish your inner light. It means being in harmony with your self, with the surrounding world, and yet living your own path, your own being."

Interjection: Freedom has external limits. We are forced to do many things, must orient ourselves on laws and regulations.

"This is an objection that often comes, and it is based on the misunderstanding about outer and inner freedom. Even in a prison cell, with a rigidly structured day and the compulsion to work without being able to live you own will, you could be free. Because this is a matter of inner freedom. When you have the feeling of freedom within you, you can also live in structures that you can accept as a result. You can shape the framework, according to your own possibilities, and your light will shines on your own path. It no longer makes any difference whether you have chosen such as condition on your own or have been forced to accept it. The life of monks in the Middle Ages was perhaps comparable to the life of someone who is in prison today. They had a fixed daily rhythm, had to do much work, slept in a little cell, moved in a little cell, and ate together in silence. In some orders they were hardly permitted to speak as well. The monks had chosen these circumstances for themselves and felt themselves free for their inner development because of the outer structures and framework.

A person in prison could feel just as free in his own situation. However, since he apparently did not make this decision on his own, he fights against it. Fighting against things that cannot be changed at the moment makes a person unfree. A battle that costs energy is created inside oneself and this creates a feeling of unwellness that restricts a person. And so there would be a possibility of achieving this inner freedom at the moment that the person in prison accepts this situation as given or even as chosen by himself. This is how everything is. Even if you live in a country where there are many freedoms, you will feel unfree when you put yourself under pressure to have to earn money or attend to certain tasks. Even in a country with much so-called freedom, people can be very unfree because they see themselves subject to obligations. Everything is relative and depends on how the individual feels about it and experiences it. Therefore, freedom is meant as inner freedom that radiates to the outside, even if it apparently looks unfree from the outside."

Interjection: Yes, should I then tolerate everything that happens to me, should I simply swallow everything and not do anything and no longer fight?

"No, this is also a misunderstanding. This is a matter of going with the flow in the inner freedom and seeing for yourself precisely what things you want to accept and what things you do not, which way you want to go and which way you do not want to go, and which framework circumstances you can change and which you cannot change, and to decide in this pattern. Freedom then arises when you become conscious that you have created your life, set your own boundaries and structures in order to experience learning steps and that you can decide yourself at any time whether you want to stay in these structures or leave them.

You can compare this with a child who goes to school. The child who feels compelled to go to school has a sense of being unfree and cannot enjoy it. However, the moment that the child decides: "I want to learn, I want to write, do math, and learn to read," it will go to school voluntarily, on the basis of its own free will, and it experiences the freedom of being able to put things to use. It knows that it has chosen these structures in order to master the learning tasks and lives in a state of inner freedom.

And although there may be no outer difference between both of these children—they go to the same school, the same class, have the same tasks—there is still a great difference inwardly.

This is a matter of creating freedom on the inside, which results in your recognition of the idea that you have created everything for yourself—your life, your existence, your structures—everything that apparently makes you unfree and that you take the responsibility for. You select and decide what you want to do, which structures you do and do not want to maintain.

Question: It isn't all that easy to understand this because the term has very strong overtones to it in other ways: What is inner freedom?

"It always turns out to be the same thing, and you will see, if you take a close look, that it is the same thing for every person. It is your own divinity, it is your own inner light, and inner freedom also means "being enlightened." This is difficult to understand as long as you do not have the necessary experience.

The difference between the individual masters is that they start from different places in order to reach the same goal, as if people wanted to go to Paris but took off from different places. And this is the same for the masters since all paths ultimately lead to enlightenment. Yet, they take different paths and work on different themes in order to get there. Inner freedom means always becoming aware of and recognizing what you have shaped and created in your own life, consciously perceiving the correlations and consciously seeing through the structures of the universe. It means manifesting and creating from this knowledge, which is something that you all do but on an unconscious level."

Question: To me, freedom means that the inner and the outer freedom come together. For me, outer freedom means that I can choose what I do on the outside. In an extreme case, inner freedom can mean that there is little I can do on the outside, as in the example of the prison. And it seems to me that someone has put themselves there on their own is a weak form of comfort. There is a feeling of outer restriction at that moment. And when I accept a job, then I must structure my day accordingly—and the great discrepancy between inner and outer freedom manifests itself for me at that moment—which then results in frustration.

"This is because you are virtually nearsighted at that moment and the parts within you are not in harmony: because in the moments when you see an apparent discrepancy between inner and outer freedom, you do not mean freedom. You mean the discrepancy between inner will and what you apparently must do. You do not look closely enough at this because human beings seldom have *one* will. There are always many parts that want something and you illuminate them to different degrees. If you, for example, want to do no work and go swimming instead, but you feel yourself forced to work, you then explain this as a lack of freedom, as having to fulfill certain structures. However, this is just an aspect of yourself that cannot be lived out at the moment since there is also that aspect within you that does exactly what it wants to do, and there are still other aspects of the will. However, you have directed your spotlight at the aspect that is contrary to the situation created on the outside. Then this appears to you as a lack of freedom.

In a state of inner freedom, you would see that there are many portions of the will within you that want a great variety of things and that you freely decide to do what you want to do. At the moment you have decided to do this and when you adjust the spotlight onto the part that wanted this, then you will be in harmony.

You can also follow another part within yourself and not work. This freedom also exists. You have this freedom, and no one can take it away from you. You have these possibilities and this freedom—and you are the one who wants to work and who has gone into these structures for this reason.

This is the interaction between the inside and the outside world. The feeling of not being free and of being pressed into structures arises when you are not in the light, not in your divinity but outside of it. It happens when you are on a level in which many contrary aspects of the will also exist that fight against each other or whose energies are exchanged, and you do not feel well with this situation. If you were in your divinity, if you were in your center, then you could freely decide and see what you want in the short term, long term, and longer term. You would have a clear view of the entire path, walking it in peace and harmony.

For many people, it is like this: They stand in Aachen and decide to go to Paris. They go over hills and through valleys, passing through musty regions and constantly quarreling with themselves. Perhaps they should have gone the other way, perhaps they should not go to Paris at all, perhaps other routes would have been better. A feeling of not being free, of being frustrated and unfulfilled arises.

When they are in their own center they know that they can choose the path. They choose the path and enjoy it since they have selected it on their own. On such a path there are naturally also junctions, situations where something else is possible. And then you once again stand at the point where you can make a choice, but you can do this on the basis of an inner peace since you know that you ultimately have already been in Paris for a long time. On the inside, you are already there where you want to be and it is the path that makes you more conscious of it. Whether you go to the left or to the right, it leads to the same goal—just with different aspects and experiences. You can go by quarreling with the situation, become unconscious and suffer, feel yourselves as victims. Or you can do this from within your inner divinity, from the feeling that you have created everything and can create everything. It is up to you: you are the ones who are going to the first grade in school and would so much like to learn algebra or integral calculus but cannot even do the multiplication table. You very much want to understand and do these things, but you lack in the fundamentals. You can visit the lessons for the 10th grade ten times and observe at these school classes, but as long as you lack in the knowledge from the 1st grade and have not yet integrated it, you will not be able to understand this calculation process.

Everything is already within you, and yet, it is still developing."

Question: Does this mean that then—when a person has inner freedom—the spotlight of attention is no longer unconsciously controlled by emotions, thoughts, and patterns but that a wide field is illuminated and one can make a decision? Can we see everything at the same time because the consciousness is greater?

"Yes, and when you have broadly illuminated the field, you can also perceive the resisting parts and accept them."

Question: Does this mean that a person can see the differences between the poles and return to the center time and again?

"You can see them and be in the center and then consciously choose which way you go because the spotlight does not change the emphasis through emotions, beliefs, and patterns."

The Meditation

Go into your belly and see a light-filled ball there. This is your divinity. This ball is still surrounded by walls, undergrowth, the entanglements of your life, and beliefs—in short, by the things that prevent the ball's light from radiating to the outside. However, you can still perceive the ball of light despite these obstacles and reach it.

Now go into the center and be in this light-filled ball, be in your divinity, and look to the outside from there. From the inside of the ball of light, look and see what is in the way of the divinity emanating to the outside world.

This meditation has two steps. You should carry out each step for a while before you go on to the next.

The first step: The ball of light has a specific size. Look at what stops this ball of light from freely radiating to all sides. Clear away these blocks, whether they are in the form of images like: "Aha, there is still a bit of wall at my left arm, I can't get through there." Then remove this wall. You can also do this be taking a close look at the blocks: "I have a meeting next week and the following fears stand in my way..."—and then transform these fears.

When you have freed the ball of light from the structures that surround it and it can radiate unhindered, the second step comes: let the ball grow, a bit more every day. Sometimes there will be days when the ball will shrink again. It is as if the ball pulsates and grows as it pulsates. Observe this and give it energy so that your ball grows and radiates to the outside into all the aura layers beyond your body.

Do a short form of this meditation every morning after you wake up, every evening before you go to sleep, and during the day when you think of it. Imagine that you have a ball of light in your center and feel how it is to "simply be." You only need a few minutes or even moments to do this, but be aware time and again that you are already in your divinity.

The Message

I greet you and send you violet light so that you cleanse and free yourselves, cleansed of the things that you are entangled and stuck in, that you hang onto. Cleanse yourselves of the old things that you drag around with you. Cleanse yourselves of whatever ties you down and makes you unfree. However, my cleansing is not a process of throwing things away, burying or getting rid of them. This cleansing is a transformation. The cleansing and freedom arise when you recognize and perceive the duality, when you integrate the duality within you and you can perceive where you stand on this barometer between black and white, between day and night, between sun and moon. They arise when you recognize that both aspects belong to this world, that both belong to life on this earth, and that growth means integrating both poles within yourself so that you can grow beyond them. Freedom means perceiving the innermost divine light, the light for which there are many names.

Let this light shine within you because when you are aware of your own innermost light, you will be free in the truth. Then you can live according to your own standards and laws since these standards and laws will be in harmony with everything. You will vibrate in the rhythm of the universe and thereby achieve the greatest freedom possible.

Some of you understand freedom to mean leaving the prison. However, this is just changing from one prison to the next, from one place to the other. True freedom occurs when you perceive, accept, and assent to both poles. When you can integrate these two poles within you and then go beyond them. And—do not misunderstand me—accepting these poles does not mean that you have to live them. Understand this using the example of the polarity of "life and death." They both exist in every moment on the earth and also within you since new cells are created and old cells die and pass away every moment. Take the example of these two extremes: accepting them and integrating them does not mean that you must experience and live death. No, this means that you recognize everything that is contained in the great wheel of life, that polarity is there, and that people wander back and forth between the poles. Perceive your inner share of the poles and integrate them into your inner life. As a result, you will be free to act according to your own innermost standards and according to your own innermost laws. You can then truly do what you consider to be right and true. And you can perceive your own truth in the light.

No. 16—Hilarion

The Universal Truth

The Effect of the Master Essence

Through the essence of *Hilarion* it is possible to perceive that the entire universe is a hologram. Everything is contained within everything else.

It strengthens the connection with the Higher Self and to higher levels of consciousness. As a result, we can recognize our place and our task within the divine plan. We see where we do not live in harmony with the lifeplan and then take steps to reinstate this harmony.

It supports us in integrating ourselves into structures without getting lost in them.

The essence also supports scientists and researchers who want to perceive correlations.

It easily brings us into changed states of consciousness, whereby it becomes possible to experience the hologram. It takes us into deep meditation and inner peace.

The essence is also suitable for people who have a mission, who are trailblazers and therefore stand alone. As a result, these people can see their task in the whole of things, integrating themselves into the universe and experiencing a sense of security (people like Wilhelm Reich and Tesla, for example).

Associated with the chakras: Forehead chakra (crown chakra)
Color: Chartreuse
Tarot card: No. 17—The Star
Gemstone: Emerald, aventurine, green double spar
Oil application: Hairline, third eye, crown chakra

A person who has balanced this aspect:
- Follows his life's goal despite all adversities and isn't influenced by other people's opinions.

- Can recognize the little things in the larger things; perceives laws like "as above, so below"; knows that he has a place in the universe, which he has already found.
- Is his own guide and master.
- Is capable of analogous thought.
- Can integrate his condition and his life into the larger correlations.
- Is open for inner inspirations and can differentiate between inspiration and his own thoughts.
- Possibly has a mission and is aware of it.

A person who has not yet balanced this aspect:
- Doesn't know where his place in life is, which task he has chosen; feels himself unwanted, excluded, and out of place.
- Feels himself separated, left alone, not a part of things; believes he doesn't have a place (in this world).
- Has no access to his own inner guide, to the Higher Self.
- Orients himself on other people; seeks guidance and truth in the outer world.
- Follows outside guides and gives up his own responsibility and truth in the process.
- Doesn't know his own truth; suppresses his inner voice; believes that what he does is what he really wants to do.
- Wants to missionize others.

The difference between No. 16—Hilarion and No. 9—Orion on the theme of "lifetask":

No. 16 brings a deep understanding for one's own lifetask and place in the larger context, in the overall picture.

No. 9 helps a person come into harmony with his own lifeplan and see a part of his path.

Description

"As above, so below" says the law of Hermes Trismegistus. This means that the laws of the macrocosm can be read in the microcosm, that the larger things are reflected in the small, that the order and truth of the cosmic realm, the universe as a whole, are reflected in life and in every person on the earth. Everything is a hologram.

The human being is the microcosm in the macrocosm. He (or she) is the likeness of the whole or—as expressed in the Bible—"was created in the image of God." The entire Creation is reflected in every individual, just as the blueprint for the entire person is contained in each cell.

The same applies to the universal truth as well. It can be found in every human being, and every person can recognize it within himself and his surrounding world. When we live in harmony with the divine, our will is in harmony with the universal truth. We do exactly what corresponds with the universal plan.

Hilarion integrates our divine aspect into our human nature. He strengthens the connection with the Higher Self, which means we can take our chosen path in life. We come into harmony with the whole and know that we translate it into action in everyday, earthly life.

Hilarion helps us recognize the hologram. He lets us understand the structures of the cosmic framework by perceiving it on the earthly level.

The whole is always in balance. Even if the individual parts change, a compensation always takes place. For example, this occurs on the earth in the movement of the air masses: when a high-pressure area builds up on the one side, a low-pressure area is created on the other side and the air masses flow from high to low.

Before we came into this life, we chose a lifeplan. Our life has a place in the universe as a whole. If the individual human being doesn't follow his lifeplan, a compensation occurs in the overall picture by another person deviating from his own plan, for example.

I illustrate this system with the following picture: Imagine a puzzle in which the individual pieces are not rigid and preformed but made of a shaking pudding (jello). Each living being has its place in this puzzle. If it takes the path in life that it has chosen for itself, the piece of the puzzle fits. However, we human beings have a free will with which we can change our puzzle form. If we deviate from our lifeplan when developing our form, the little piece of the puzzle no longer fits exactly into the provided place. Since the other pieces aren't rigid either, they change their form and the entire picture is created anew. However, this is a new picture with room for the deviating piece.

No matter what we do, how we act, whether we follow our lifeplan or not, we have a place in the universe and belong to it. We are and remain a part of the whole, even if we change our form. This is God's unconditional love. Our deviation doesn't impair the whole but it does impair our life. We receive increasingly clear indications that we are no longer following the lifeplan that we have chosen, as has already been described using the example of illness.

A person who uses the essence will take a look at the parts of his life in which he does not follow his lifeplan, the areas that he has previously suppressed and didn't want to see. He sees blocks that have hindered him up to now in becoming aware of them. Under certain circumstances, this creates resistance that expresses itself as anger, aggression, fatigue, sadness, a sense of unwellness, and perhaps also as confusion. This is because the part that doesn't want to look at things and doesn't want to see what has been suppressed continues to exit. However, through the essence the inner eye is directed precisely at them.

One person who used the *Hilarion* Essence felt an anger against himself as a result. He realized how much he had given in when involved in confrontations in the past because he believed this was the more sensible way to act. Because of difference of opinion in his profession, he had ultimately changed companies a number of times. As a result of the essence, he became aware that he had acted against his own best interests over and over again, which got him into the same difficulties. It was high time for him to learn to remain in his place and represent his own truth.

A person who has selected the *Hilarion* Essence is prepared to find his individuality and his task, experiencing everything and himself within it. He is willing to understand the universal truth.

The essence of *Hilarion* brings us into changed states of consciousness and strengthens the ability to make contact with everything else because of a sense of solidarity (from out of the hologram).

It brings us into deep mediation and inner peace. While *Lao Tse* leads us to peace within ourselves, *Hilarion* brings us to peace within the universe as a whole. The limitations of the "self" can fall away. We experience that we are integrated in the cosmos and have a place within the divine whole. We experience how we belong to the divine existence. And our aura expands.

The experience of belonging is particularly healing for people who feel themselves to be separated and who believe that they have no place.

The Meditation

Sit in the lotus position or imagine that you are sitting in it and feel your third eye. Sense how it feels, what it looks like, how wide it is open, how far it expands, and what color it has. Then perceive your crown chakra at the center of your head. How far does it extend upwards? What color does it have? Then imagine how the crown chakra connects with your Higher Self, the universal cosmic law, or the universal cosmic truth, God's truth and love. Next, let the energy of the Higher Self flow into your crown chakra. Pay attention to the color that this energy has. It may change from meditation to meditation.

Let this light flow through your crown chakra into your third eye and see how your third eye begins to rotate, to open, and how far this bright cosmic light around you expands. It radiates to the front and to the back.

Let this energy flow to the throat chakra, which opens to the front and to the back as a result, and also radiates the white light into your aura.

The same thing happens in the heart chakra, in the 3rd chakra, the 2nd chakra, and the 1st chakra. Finally, this light flows through your legs, into your knees, into your feet, and into the ground.

When the light has reached the floor, a path opens up—a path that is clear and bright. It is your path in life. Walk along this path and look at what you encounter on the path and at the edge of the path to the right and to the left. You can choose whether you want to go further into the future, whether we walk through the present, or whether you wander in the past.

Take your path in life and when you encounter things that you can heal, heal them by letting cosmic light flow into them.

At the end of the meditation, see yourself sitting in the lotus position again in front of the path that you have taken.

The Message

Some of you have lost the path, the path of living your own life and your own truth. And you are not happy as a result and often cannot cope in this world and in this life. Something is missing on the inside and on the outside. Perhaps they will notice this because of their illnesses, because of the things that do not succeed in their lives, or because of their inner state, the unpleasant thoughts and feelings. They are missing something.

What they are missing is their own light, is the path on which they can wander, on which they can return home.

I support you in opening your eyes, in once again recognizing the outer eyes and the inner eyes, the light and the path. I support you so that you will see which path is your own, so that you do not take the wrong paths or follow guides who are not true guides, who do not bring you to your selves, to your own strength and wisdom but attempt to make you dependent on them and darken your own light. I bring you clarity on your path because whoever sees light on his path can more easily take this path, even if there are difficulties.

My energy is the clear power that leads people on their path, on the path of the truth, and the path of living in harmony with your own universal laws, with your own inner law.

I make you clear and true. I connect you with the cosmic universal laws, with your own inner truth, with the laws of your divinity. I bring you into harmony with your path. And with my energy, you will go with strong steps, illuminated by your own inner light, as if you were carrying a lamp that shows you the path.

You receive clarity and perceive what your truth and the universal truth is. You perceive the cosmic laws with which you want to live in harmony. And you perceive that you are a part of the divine whole.

No. 17—*Pallas Athene*

Joy and Abundance

The Effect of the Master Essence

The essence of *Pallas Athene* opens the perception for the feelings of the moment (for example, emotions, inner images, and intuition) and helps us communicate and live them out. At the same time, blocks are dissolved that have prevented us from expressing ourselves creatively through writing, singing, dancing, playing an instrument, or painting.

It allows the vital energy and joy in life to once again bubble.

It connects logic with intuition, analytical and analogous thinking, also connecting the right and left halves of the brain.

This essence brings us into contact with inner wealth, with our own potential and the abundance of the universe.

It supports the healing of our inner child.

It is also suitable for artists in order to give form to their ideas and creativity.

Associated with the chakras: Heart chakra (throat chakra)
Color: Gold-pink
Tarot card: No. 3—The Empress
Gemstone: Opal
Oil application: 7th cervical vertebra, shoulders (zone of fear, see pg. 94), stomach, as well as: spinal column from bottom to top, upper edge of ankle, and outer edge of feet

A person who has balanced this aspect:
- Is full of the joy of life.
- Enjoys self-expression.
- Spontaneously expresses his feelings.
- Lives his creativity and finds ways of expressing it and giving it form.
- Lives in order and structure without falling prey to rigidity.
- Behaves in a naturally self-secure manner.
- Lives a natural, playful sexuality.

- Experiences the world with childish curiosity, openness, and astonishment.
- Lets the inner wealth become visible and lets others participate in it.

A person who has not yet balanced this aspect:
- Is an excessively serious, grim, and rigid individual.
- Lives according to rigid principles and structures: "this has to be done": is constricted and caught up in his own desires.
- Has stiff movements and manners.
- Has a stubborn opinion; is mentally inflexible.
- Has strict self-discipline: denies himself pleasures because he clings to principles and overdoes them.
- Is inhibited when it comes to self-expression.
- Has little access to abilities of the right half of the brain—potential, art, and personal artistic expression.
- Lives in the consciousness of poverty and a feeling of need; is stingy because he believes that everything is limited so he isn't permitted to deal with things in a lavish way.

But also a person who:
- Lives without structure and order; is chaotic.
- Is stuck in childishness.

The difference between No. 17—Pallas Athene and No. 3—El Morya on the theme of "self-expression":

No. 17 opens the access to potential and ability to be expressive.
No. 3 dissolves the "fear of failure."
No. 19 helps in no longer hiding the abilities, giving us the courage to show them.

The difference between No. 17—Pallas Athene and No. 4—Kwan Yin on the theme of "expressing feelings":

No. 17 helps spontaneously express the momentary feelings.
No. 4 dissolves old, pent-up, and blocked feelings, opens the access to the emotions.

Description

On the first day that we began to work with *Pallas Athene*, I experienced another world. I had woken up early in the morning, the sun was just rising, and I felt awake, well, and full of joy. Nothing could hold me in bed, and I decided to take a walk. The world appeared new to me. I saw glittering dewdrops hanging in spider webs, the colors of the sunrise, the birds warbled sweeter song on this morning than before, and the stream along which I walked sang a completely different melody. Like an amazed child, I saw nature with completely new eyes. Then I discovered a beautiful spot that I had never seen before, although I had lived in the area for two years already. During the walk I sang, and verses came into my mind. This inner joy accompanied me for the entire day.

The experience shows quite clearly the effect of *Pallas Athene*. She makes us aware of the beauty and joy that surrounds us and is within us. It is the natural joy of life that children also show when they laugh spontaneously and run with exuberant energy; the liveliness of the dolphins that jump out of the water and do a somersault. This joy of life is an expression of freely flowing vital energy.

The essence also allows us to become aware of what prevents us from always living joyfully. Perhaps we remember situations from childhood in which we were stopped in our liveliness or had suppressed our own vital energy and bubbly joy ourselves. This can trigger sadness. It may be that we withdraw and let the tears flow—just like a child does. The inner child heals its pain.

This was experienced by a girlfriend who came into contact with this sad inner child during the first days of using the essence. Sometimes she cried like a child, and sometimes she was also defiant. Then, with increasing frequency, the playful, cheerful, natural child shone through. The more the wounds of the inner child healed, the more cheerful, exuberant, and playful she became.

Unpleasant experiences and dreams of childhood and the prenatal period also heal, and feelings and emotions can once again be expressed spontaneously.

Natural playfulness and joy can also be lived in sexuality.

In Greek mythology, *Pallas Athene* is the Goddess of Art, Science, Peace, and the Home. The energy of *Pallas Athene* therefore promotes both scientific approaches and analytical thinking, as well as creative expression in every sense. She strengthens the connection between logic and intuition and the right and left halves of the brain (intuition, sensory perception, holistic thinking and comprehension are associated with the right half of the brain, and logic, analysis, reading, writing, and calculating with the left half of the brain). As a result, the inner perceptions can be more easily understood and expressed.

Not only artists are inspired as result and can better give form to the inner creative processes—we also become more successful in expressing ourselves in daily life. We more easily find the words in conversations, we express our inner state while singing, and we show our inner experiences through dance. We give expression to what we feel right now, what moves us at the moment, through singing, dancing, painting, writing, and playing instruments. In the process, we also find our own natural self-assurance.

Through the essence we acquire access to our potential, to abilities that we carry within us but haven't yet put to use or haven't had the confidence to demonstrate them. We find our own inner riches and our own abundance, discovering that true wealth comes from within. We recognize this in nature: a fruit tree bears one-hundred times more blossoms than fruit and every plant produces much more seeds than it requires for its reproduction. Everywhere we look in nature, we find abundance and surplus. Mother Nature teaches us generosity—she is an expression of life. We also have more abilities and potentials within us than what we live out.

Every individual who is truly rich on the inside lets others participate in this wealth. Those who live in abundance like to share. Every type of clinging originates in the fear of lack and expresses a consciousness of poverty.

Pallas Athene also helps us confront the material side of life. She makes us aware of our limiting beliefs regarding "living in abundance."

Pallas Athene is also the Goddess of the Home, providing order and structure. However, she doesn't do this in a rigid, fixed way; the order serves the well-being of human beings and the

structure gives support without constricting. The essence therefore also helps in providing structure for taking creative action.
It helps comprehend, analyze, and understand situations. And it
also helps in breaking out of rigid, bogged-down situations.

The Meditation

Take a walk and be aware of the surrounding world. Pay attention to the riches of Mother Nature. For example, stroll through
a meadow of fruit trees in spring and look at the trees with their
thousands and thousands of blossoms and the thousands of bees
that come to collect nectar, for example.

In autumn, look at the fruit on these trees—the cherries, apples, and plums—and see how the trees hang full of them.

Or imagine a river or walk along one and see how the water
flows in abundance, how the melody sings in a merry and joyful
way, and how it jumps over stones, bubbles and laughs. See
how the sun is reflected and the water glitters and glows as if
gold and diamonds were sparkling in it.

On a moonlit night, look at a lake and how it seems to be
made of silver. Let yourself be caught up in the beauty of nature,
its sounds and fragrances. Pay attention to every detail.

Find other images of abundance and wealth in nature.

Then see your own life and remember situations of joy and
happiness.

Afterwards, imagine a rose bush covered with buds. Become
this rose bush and imagine how your branches are filled with
rose buds, blossoming and blossoming, one after the other. Each
bud bursts open and exudes its fragrance, followed by the next
and the next one until the bush is covered with roses. Recognize
in this way that you yourself are full of wealth and abundance
and can live in joy.

Let the pink-golden light of *Pallas Athene* flow into yourself.
Become a flower in your color, and let the roots grow deep into
the earth. See the stem, the leaves, and the blossoms.

Next, encounter your favorite animal in your thoughts. Play
with it and learn from it. Change yourself into the creature that
you like and admire.

Then return to your human existence.

The Message

I send you the light of joy, of abundance and wealth. Realize that the song of joy and abundance resonates in Mother Nature around you, within yourselves, in life, in being, and in the cosmos.

You humans live on a planet full of riches and beauty. With "riches" I do not mean just the material wealth that you consider valuable but also the abundance that prevails on the earth in every area. You always have enough air available to you, and you breathe this air every day. Without it you would die. There are great numbers of trees that once again cleanse this air. There is water that allows you to live, that satisfies your thirst, that composes 70% of you, and that flows through your world of nature.

Wealth and beauty surround you, and so you should become involved and open yourselves. Go into this wealth and beauty and expect the beauty, the light, and the love with my energy.

And begin to perceive what is around you and what happens within yourselves.

Also look to see what situations of scarcity still exist in your life and begin to transform them by filling them with what you need. Take an exact look at what you need so that you feel yourselves full, round, and fulfilled, so that you are warm and can pass on the joy and the abundance.

I, *Pallas Athene*, accompany you and show you your inner beauty, the beauty of being one, of merging with everything—your own blossoming. I show you the world through the eyes of beauty and love. It is dance, it is music, it is jubilation, it is joy and celebration, no matter whether there is rain or sunshine, whether it is winter or summer. No matter whether you stand on the bridge or on the mountain, the joy is within you and the rejoicing is within you. Begin to celebrate with me. Enjoy life and your inner light. Let your inner light shine like gold and immerse your life and your being in golden light. Melt the warm golden flames of this sun into yourselves and become one.

This is how you set out on the path of recognizing your places of barrenness, deficiency, and hunger so that you can fill them and so that you can blossom. This will help you give that rose within you the necessary nourishment so that it blossoms and can unfold, presenting its beauty over a wide expanse so that people turn around and admire this rose. It attracts your attention and you yourself sense the desire to also become such a rose.

No. 18—*Lady Portia*

Being Balanced

The Effect of the Master Essence

The energy of *Lady Portia* centers us, brings us into a state of balance and inner equilibrium, and lets us find our own center at every moment and in every way.

It supports our inner stability and equilibrium and balances between extremes. This applies to both the mental and spiritual, as well as the physical level.

It creates a balance between the earthly aspects and the divine aspects.

Associated with the chakras: Heart chakra (base chakra and crown chakra)
Color: Coral (salmon)
Tarot card: No. 8—Justice (Adjustment)
Gemstone: Rutile quartz, malachite, green apophyllite
Oil application: 2nd chakra, around the navel, sacral vertebra

A person who has balanced this aspect:
- Is stable, in his inner center, harmonious; doesn't let anything rob him of his inner peace and equilibrium, even when everything around him is complete chaos.
- Has a conciliatory aura that causes other people to calm down as well.
- Doesn't let anything shake him up.
- Quickly regains his harmoniousness if he loses it.
- Is secure in making decisions and taking action.
- Is balanced in his opinion.
- Is open for experiences of the opposing side.
- Is open for opinions of others; can always reorient himself and finds the way back to his center time and again.
- Considers and weighs both sides before making decisions.
- Can easily create harmony.
- Lives in inner peace.

A person who has not yet balanced this aspect:
- Vacillates excessively in all areas.
- Experiences strong emotional fluctuations.
- Easily lets himself be made to feel insecure and thrown off his center by the outside world.
- Can't make decisions or has a difficult time doing so; is fickle and indecisive.
- Always has the feeling of not having made the right decision or of having made a hollow compromise when he has decided on something; or accepts other people's decisions because he can't decide on his own, but also feels uneasy about doing so.
- Constantly carries on inner dialogues.
- Is full of doubts.
- Excludes experiences and parts of the world; is often stuck in one extreme and sees only one side of the coin.
- Supports an extreme ideology and fights against other views; is fanatic.
- Always supports the same opinion in discussions; persists in one extreme.
- Makes hollow compromises.
- Has an unsteady, insecure way of walking since he doesn't have his physical center at the middle of his body.

Description

The world is a world of polarity: day and night, black and white, good and evil, yin and yang, masculine and feminine, giving and taking, joy and sadness, and war and peace. Both poles together form a unity. Only when both poles exist can the differences be perceived and valued. Only when we experience disagreeable things do we start to look for what is pleasant in life.

The poles appear to stand in incompatible opposition to each other and challenge us to find the balance. We are the farthest away from being "whole" and having inner harmony precisely when we are stuck in one extreme. Yet, the path to becoming whole, to inner balance and harmony, only succeeds when the other pole is accepted as well. In this sense, no human being is just good or just evil and we all bear feminine and masculine aspects within ourselves. An integration of both parts leads to living together more harmoniously and to healing.

A person who has lived too long in one extreme, who has gone too far in one direction like a pendulum, often first swings in the opposite direction, in the other extreme, before he finds the balance. For example, people who have primarily lived out the masculine qualities of vigor, logical thought, distance, and initiative, often experience a phase of intuition, strong emotions and moods, premonitions, dreams, and visions on the path to integration.

The work with *Lady Portia*'s energy supports precisely this process. She helps us in accepting, experiencing, and integrating the previously rejected pole. She helps us create a balance.

Only when both poles are in harmony can we freely choose. Then we can decide where we want to go and what we want to do. Then we can choose our momentary standpoint and are no longer stuck in one aspect because we reject the other side. Our possibilities and variations expand. And we experience that there is an individual center. Not every person achieves the same standpoint on the path between the poles.

Being in equilibrium means living an inner harmony, balance, inner peace, and a sense of being centered.

Centering yourself physically and psychologically means finding an inner point of reference that gives you stability.
DOLORES KRIEGER

One woman who used the essence had just experienced a separation and felt shattered because of it. She couldn't decide what she should now do, whether she should work in her old profession again, give further seminars, or if she should first be concerned with herself. She had met a new man and didn't know whether she should get involved again or first spend time alone. After she had taken the *Lady Portia* Essence for a while, she developed an inner composure, an inner peace, and was able to make the decisions easily. Yet, at the same time she knew that she could change her opinion and take new paths when the choice that she had made no longer appealed to her.

On the path to harmony, it's important to trust, to consciously look at the path, and to recognize that the inner balance is learned be falling out of the center time and again and then finding it anew. Life frequently gives us momentum in a different direction. Unpleasant experiences, emotional traumas, or physical shocks can throw us off balance. As a result, we remain in motion like a scale. Being in equilibrium means coming back into balance, to our center, after each time the scales waver.

As soon as we are at the center, the door opens to the inner light, to another state of consciousness. There we acquire access to intuition and inner wisdom, finding peace and strength. We have the strength to remain in a state of inner balance, even if everything around us is in complete chaos. The things that used to shake us up then appear to no longer touch us.

A person who is at his own center is completely present.

And the earthly and divine aspects of our being are connected at the center.

A person who has his physical center of gravity in the middle of the body can also remain centered more easily in the emotional and mental areas. The following exercise can support this effect:

Stand up straight, your legs spread at about the width of the shoulders and feet parallel. Your physical center of gravity is located in the floor of the pelvis. Then start to slowly and consciously shift your weight to one side. Next, change the direction and shift your weight to the other side. Pay exact attention to the center point: when do you reach it and when do you go beyond it?

If you repeat this exercise for a while, it will be easier for you to come into meditation and also be more stable in everyday life.

The Meditation

Imagine you are a ball on a string that swings back and forth and increasingly returns to the center.

Or choose a situation from your life in which you fluctuate between two sides. Then imagine again that you are the ball that swings back and forth between these two poles. When this happens, you may perceive how this center could take concrete form in your life.

The Message

Sometimes people first have to swing to the other pole in order to reach the middle and maintain a balance once again, just like a pendulum that has gone too far to one side.

Trust the process—the pendulum will swing back to the center. Even if you become alarmed on the path between the poles—trust. From life to life, you go from one pole to the next, and in this life you also wander back and forth between the poles. This is why I support you in finding your way back to the center within yourselves. From this point at the center, you can freely decide. Within your own center you can choose, you can freely take action, you are connected with your own innermost wisdom and intuition.

You human beings sometimes love to swing back and forth between the extremes. And sometimes you lean out very far. Then you have a hard time returning back to your own center. The game of the pendulum, the swinging back and forth, is an exercise for you. You learn where your limits are, you taste the duality in all of its aspects. You train in reaching your own center time and again. If you have gone too far beyond your own center, it is difficult for you to return there again. So you should be aware of this when you move back and forth. Recognize what point you are at when you fall out of your center, and how you can reach it again.

The door into another dimension opens at the center. When you are at the center, you have enough stability, you are connected enough with the earth in order to experience this dimension. A tree can also only grow to a great height when it is rooted well enough in the earth.

I support you in coming into your center, in being at your center, and maintaining stability there. Then the door will open into a new dimension.

No. 19—Helion

Being Like the Sun

The Effect of the Master Essence

The essence of Helion supports us in visibly showing our own character. It makes us aware of what has stopped us from having a charismatic aura up to now.

It connects the unconditional love of the whole with the love for one's self. As a result, we come to self-love and our inner light shines.

It supports meditation.

Associated with the chakras: Heart chakra (hara, throat chakra)
Color: Yellow-gold of the sun
Tarot card: No. 19—The Sun
Gemstone: Sunstone, golden topaz
Oil application: Chest area in front and back, beneath the collarbone (zone of fear, see page 96)

A person who has balanced this aspect:
- Has integrated love and strength.
- Possesses natural authority and a charismatic aura.
- Is conscious of his inner light, shows and lives it.
- Attracts other people through his appearance and his sense of self-expression; is authentic.
- Lets others participate in his inner light.

A person who has not yet balanced this aspect:
- Holds back or hides his inner light and the radiance of his personality.
- Hides himself; is inconspicuous; doesn't show and live his abilities and inner greatness; isn't authentic.
- Knows his inner qualities but believes they aren't worth anything and wants to have everything from the outside.

- Plays ignorant to the outside world, as if he doesn't know what to do with what he has experienced or doesn't perceive anything.
- Acts unimpressed and untouched to the outside world; listens to things with an expressionless face.
- Can hide his own experiencing so deeply within himself that he loses access to it himself.
- Prefers to talk about others but not about himself.

Description

A person who has found his inner equilibrium and is at his center recognizes his own innermost light. There at the center is the source of his own light, which is connected with the divine source. *Lady Portia* leads us to the center; *Helion* supports us in letting our light shine to the outside world.

One woman who used the essence reported that several days after its application she was approached by people in order to work with her, win her over for new projects, and who even offered money for the projects. Her personal magnetism had become powerful and winning.

After another woman, who managed a dog-grooming salon, used the essence she was asked time and again by customers whether she had a new hairstyle or had she changed something about herself because she looked so good. The dogs also showed a reaction—they became calmer and let themselves be groomed more easily.

Sometimes we encounter people who have a charismatic aura. We believe that they were born with it or we say that they are very special people and admire them. When this happens, we do nothing other than take our eyes off of our own light and believe that we can't do this ourselves. We believe that we ourselves don't have such a light or such a potential and that we are too weak or incapable to develop such personal magnetism. However, this is just our trick for stopping ourselves from living our own potential.

Our deepest fear is not that we are inadequate.
Our deepest fear is that we are immensely powerful.
It is our light that we fear, not our darkness.
NELSON MANDELA

A person who has a charismatic personality can't hide it. People look at him or look up to him, use him as a father figure or mother figure, give him authority, and surrender their own responsibility. They subordinate themselves and put him on a "pedestal," and then try to push him back down from the pedestal upon which they themselves have placed this personality. We fear that the same thing will happen to us when we let our light penetrate to the outside world. We suddenly become visible and can no longer hide ourselves. People suddenly want to be led by us—sometimes just so they can have a guilty party in case something goes wrong.

Many people probably suffer from these fears—and overcoming them is an important step!

Helion supports us in developing our own inner light. This light also the contains strength to deal with the reactions of the surrounding world. It is the love for ourselves, the love of the whole, of God, that lets us shine. It is unconditional self-love, the love of the self.

The essence of *Helion* lets us see what stops us from letting our light shine to the outside world and why we hide behind the masks with which we identify ourselves after a certain amount of time. The masks prevent too much inner light from penetrating to the outside. They protect us, yet constrict us at the same time. We no longer need this type of protection when our light shines.

The Meditation

Imagine that you are the sun of this planetary system. This sun shines beyond all the boundaries and the rays reach even the last corner of the cosmos, although this happens many, many years later.

And so imagine that you are the sun and let your energy stream out, out of your innermost self, out of your center, out of your being. Let the sunbeams flow to the earth and envelop it. See that there is always one side that is bright and filled with light and one side that is dark. Envelop the bright side of the earth with the light. Let the light penetrate the earth, illuminate the atmosphere, the organisms, the animals and plants, the stones, the water, and the human beings. Everything on the earth accepts the sunlight, and many people take it for granted. It is a gift, but at the same time it is not a gift.

With this sunlight meditation, you can experience what it means to be a sun. And when you have experienced this, see yourself as a human sun. Imagine that you walk through a department store, through a crowd of people, see yourself at other places, and let your innermost being shine like the sun while you do this. The more you see yourself shine or other people see you shine, the more you will open yourself and the greater the gleam of light will be to the outside world. Many people will approach you and things will happen that had not been possible for you before. They happen through the sun in your innermost self.

Then imagine past situations, how they would have been had you let this sun within you shine.

The Message

I greet you, you people on the earth who often live in darkness and shadows. I greet you with my rays and my sun-like being so that you also discover and develop the part within you that is like the sun, that is light. Find your center and then look to see what and where the sun is within your body, your sun, and let this sun shine.

Develop yourselves, you human beings, so that you will also be like the sun and the earth will become bright. And see that the shadows are also a part of everything on this earth.

I support you in bringing your sun-like being out of the darkness so that you sparkle and shine, warm yourselves on your own light, light the path for others, and continue to be visible. Shine like the sun that bears heat and warmth within itself and radiates purely for its own joy far beyond its boundaries. So many living beings and planets profit from it. This is how it is and yet it is not its intention. It warms and radiates because of so much joy, it gives life and supports growth.

And so I also bring you to your inner sun, your sun that shines in your heart, in your hara, in your entire being. Your own sun opens you up, lets you become warm and clear—clear for your own path.

No. 20—*Aeolus*

Recognizing the Creator Within Ourselves

The Effect of the Master Essence

The essence of Aeolus connects with consciousness and creative power. It strengthens the connection with the Higher Self. It connects the strength of the divine source with the earthly strength in the creative process, thereby supporting affirmation techniques and the power of thought.

It promotes holistic vision and develops the perception of the third eye. As a result, creativity is possible in harmony with the whole.

This essence connects with the 8th chakra and brings us into deep meditation.

Associated with the chakras: Forehead chakra (crown and base chakra)
Color: Turquoise
Tarot card: No. 20—Judgment (The Aeon)
Gemstone: Fluorite, quartz crystal
Oil application: Third eye (= forehead chakra), 7th cervical vertebra, crown chakra; as well as inner side of ankle.

A person who has balanced this aspect:

- Possesses consciousness and has experienced the state of "being conscious"; knows the difference between this and the normal state, which the enlightened masters call the state of sleep or world of illusion.
- Sees through the world of illusion; uses the world and other people as a mirror ("as it is on the inside, so it is on the outside").
- Perceives the correlation between thoughts, feelings, and what happens in the outside world.
- Is aware of his creative power and applies it.
- Creates his life from a state of abundance, in harmony with the universal laws, and from a love of existence.

- Is conscious of his thoughts and feelings.
- Can easily go into his subconscious mind and bring things to light.
- Possesses a high level of permeability between the levels of consciousness.

A person who has not yet balanced this aspect:
- Believes that he is a victim; believes that he can't change anything, that he is helplessly at the mercy of the game of life.
- Believes that the world is like he sees it; lives with a worm's-eye view
- Attempts to use his power of thought for manipulative purposes.

The difference between No. 20—Aeolus and No. 6—Djwal Khul on the theme of "being a victim":

No. 20   strengthens particularly when a person believes that he is at the mercy of the greater whole; intensifies strength on the basis of being connected with the whole.

No. 6   strengthens particularly when a person believes he is too weak and has no strength of his own; supports the belief in one's own strength.

Description

Just like *Dwal Khul*, *Aeolus* also teaches us that we are the creators of our life. We perceive the creative power that leads to the creation of the world and also exists inside of us. *Aeolus* connects consciousness, strength, access to the divine source, and earthly strength with each other. He lets us take practical steps. Through this energy, it is possible to consciously create our life and do the right things at the proper time in harmony with the universal truth. We can free ourselves from the darkness of unconsciousness. As creators, we assume responsibility for our life.

We clearly recognize the correlation between what we think, what we fear, and what happens. Many people have already had this experience of having a thought that came true a short time later. Above all, this occurs with the negative fears: "I hope the child doesn't let the bottle fall," we think and already see it falling in our mind's eye—and then the bottle falls. These correlations are disastrous when they are seen as confirmation of a supposed premonition: for example, we expect that our neighbor doesn't greet us and is unfriendly (and unconsciously react in such a way that he does this), the neighbor doesn't greet us (*we* created it this way), and we say: "I already knew it."

Aeolus lets us perceive such correlations, lets us recognize what we create and how we create it. As a result, it opens up the possibility of more consciously observing our thoughts and feelings and connecting them with what happens. We recognize what it means to *be conscious*, how we perceive this state within us, how we use it, and when we forget it again. He teaches us to pay attention to our thoughts, to observe how the thoughts drift by, and to see what we create in every moment. It is therefore also possible to bring thoughts and feelings into harmony.

During the time in which a man worked with the *Aeolus* Essence, he was an exhibitor at a trade fair. He heard about a party to given by another exhibitor and wanted to be invited to it. This didn't appear to work out at first, but a few hours before it began he met someone who invited him to the party—without him even having mentioned his desire to go to it. The party took place at a remote location, and since he didn't have a car, he created the situation that someone took him along and that he found someone who took him back to his apartment afterwards, which was about 60 kilometers away. He then found someone who took him along to the party and at the party he met two people whose way home went past his door. One of them took him along and let him out at his front door.

Another person who used the essence wrote me: "The effect of the *Aeolus* Essence is illuminating and relieving. It's really possible to see how my life develops out of my innermost self and how I create my own experiences. In the past few days, at least three situations occurred that I had thought about or felt just hours beforehand. A great lightness about life as a creative game has grown within me—like a laughing puppeteer."

We recognize that everything we create is a learning step and mirror of our own inner situation. When we compare the present with what we have thought and expected in the past, we can comprehend these correlations. When we take the step from the unconscious to consciousness, we become the creator of our own life. For this purpose, we use both the cosmic powers and energies, as well as the earthly powers. Only when both are in harmony, when energy and matter work together does the thought materialize.

Those who create from divinity, from the harmony with the whole, create from abundance and love and not from desire or "hunger," fear, and worry. They create not against the divine order but as divine co-creators in harmony with the whole.

The energy of *Aeolus* supports holistic sight and opens the perception of the third eye for inner processes and for another type of "seeing." We can leave our worm's-eye perspective, come into contact with our Higher Self, and observe other areas of consciousness and occurrences from an overall perspective. As a result, we also succeed in seeing larger areas and achieve a deeper understanding. We recognize what has fallen out of the harmonious state of togetherness, what disturbs the harmony of body, mind, and soul, and perceive the pending steps of integration.

It is much easier for us to achieve the stillness of meditation and contact with other levels of consciousness and dimensions with this energy. And it intensifies the contact with the 8th chakra, which is found outside of our body, about 50 centimeters above the head.

We have experiences that can be difficult to explain with the mind and with words. At the same time, we know what should be done and how we should proceed. The mind may question all of this and have its doubts, but a deep inner knowledge also exists along with these doubts that supports us. So we will be at the right place at the proper time and meet the right people.

The Meditation

Go into your center to your inner light. Then let this white or white-golden light flow through your entire body, into every layer, every organ, all the bones, and every cell. What is still in darkness within you becomes light as a result.

Afterwards, let your light flow into your chakras and the layers of your aura.

During each step, perceive what happens.

The Message

I greet you. You humans know that you bear the immortal part within yourselves, that you are the immortal part within yourselves, and that this part is godlike, similar to the Creator. And so you also live this aspect upon the earth, usually unconsciously, and yet you live it every day and in every minute. With every thought you create your life and everything associated with it. Sometimes this even includes things with a far-reaching scope.

So it is an important step on the path to unity to perceive that you are similar to the Creator and that you create in your surrounding world, in your life, and here on this earth. It is important for you to recognize what strength and power you have and thereby perceive the responsibility for yourselves and for your lives so that you can consciously shape your lives. To truly grasp and understand this is a long-lasting process. So takes a look at this aspect. Look to see what thoughts you have, and become conscious of the correlation between your powers of thought and what happens. Become aware that you create more than you want to perceive. And perceive that you have the key to shaping your lives. For this reason, I support you in recognizing the correlations between the inside and the outside, in looking through the veil of reality, and seeing into the depths of the self.

No. 21—Mary

Perceiving the Unity

The Effect of the Master Essence

The essence of *Mary* connects us with overall existence and with divine love. As a result, it is possible to let the "motherly," giving love from the source and abundance flow without becoming powerless.

We recognize that we have always been connected with divine love, and have always been in unity. Heaven and earth merge and we become one.

It makes us aware that everything is interwoven with the divine and that matter is a vessel for the divine soul.

It lets us perceive in which areas we feel ourselves to be separate or act as if we didn't live in unity.

The essence brings us into deep meditation and makes it possible for us to experience the state of being one.

Associated with the chakras: All of them
Color: Dark magenta (mixture of blue and violet)
Tarot card: No. 21—The World (The Universe)
   and No. 0—The Fool
Gemstone: White and pink diamond
Oil application: Around the navel, on the third eye, 7th cervical
   vertebra, and pulse on the wrist; additionally on the crown chakra.

A person who has balanced this aspect:
• Feels himself connected with everything; is a drop in the ocean; lives in the consciousness of unity and therefore has access to all of being.
• Perceives his divine soul.
• Has experienced the principle of divine, all-encompassing love.
• Has an open heart and is connected with all human beings in love.
• Lives the aspect of the "nurturing mother" as a positive principle.

A person who has not yet balanced this aspect:
- Feels himself separate, left alone by existence, outcast and inwardly empty.
- Experiences the pain of separation.
- Often has the feeling of being unwanted and not truly loved.
- Easily feels himself to be excluded, isolated, and unloved; suffers greatly from fears of loss.
- Gives much and likes to do so, but overexerts himself in the process and is disappointed by other people's reaction.

Description

In many religions, a virginal female figure connects the divine with the earthly. In Christianity she is called Mary. Mary is the symbol for pure matter.

Modern science—quantum physics—has shown us that matter isn't a solid mass but also made of vibration, as is light—matter just vibrates more densely. *Mary* then symbolizes pure matter, which is capable of accepting the divine vibration and accepts it. She is therefore a symbol of humanity since the human being is also made of matter. The body is the matter which connects itself with the divine vibration, the immortal soul. Like every human being and every form of existence, *Mary* is the vessel that accepts the divine vibration, bears it, and gives birth to it in this world. This essence strengthens us in the task of letting the divine become visible in the earthly dimension and living our divine aspect in earthly life.

Not only human beings are a connection between matter and divine energy: every form of being on the earth is also shaped in this way. Everything is interwoven with this universal energy. As a result, we are connected with everything else. The divine energy is one. It cannot be separated, although it apparently appears in single individuals and although people, animals, plants, and minerals are apparently distinct from each other. Yet, this is the "reality of the human eye, human duality." When we can see beyond this, we experience that everything is one and nothing is separate.

> *The true illusion is*
> *that we are separate.*
> RON SMOTHERMON

These statements are found time and again in the teachings of spiritual masters and esoteric wisdom. It can be read and heard, yet we still cannot understand it through the rational mind. Only those who have experienced and felt this truth can understand and comprehend it. And then it is difficult to express it in words. The listener cannot understand if he hasn't had a similar experience himself. The statements about the effect of the *Mary* Essence like that it "opens the heart and we are connected with all human beings in love" may perhaps sound rather superficial or pithy for many people. Yet, those who have experienced it will know what this means.

We experience the connecting love through the *Mary* Essence. It takes us beyond the consciousness of the self, the ego of the individual, for moments since the ego is what separates us from existence. The ego is the fence in the landscape that separates us from the whole yet cannot truly divide up the land. The *Mary* Essence lets us feel time and again that we are connected, that we always have been and will be connected with everything.

We often experience how people get startled when they hear these sentences. It may be that they are afraid of "dissolving," that the drop disappears in the ocean and they disappear along with it. Or they may believe that there is no more liveliness in the state of oneness, that everything is motionless and empty. Whatever it may be, we have much resistance within us that stops us from undermining and dissolving the borders making us an individual. The thought often frightens us.

In the world of duality, the path to unity leads through polarity. So our path to unity is often connected with separation and the pain of separation (birth, puberty, death...) The idea of unity and oneness often triggers memories of the pain of separation, which we carry within ourselves. The transition in time and space, into this earthly world, creates within us the experience of being cut off from the whole, from unity, from divine love. We bear this pain within us, just like the longing to connect ourselves with the divine source once again. And precisely this pain lets us search for the unity. When we heal this pain and dissolve the illusion of separation, we are in the unity and we are in all-encompassing love.

When a couple with whom we are friends began using the *Mary* Essence, precisely this pain of separation became the central theme. Completely unexpectedly, the man fell in love with another woman and separated from his partner. He believed that he had found a motherly, nurturing love and sense of security with the other woman that he hadn't received from his mother. Our girlfriend went through the pain of separation and "remembered" similar situations in her life, past experiences of separation. The feeling of being alone and misunderstood arose as it had during puberty and the pain of being a small child—the times she was in her little bed alone and felt deserted. She once again lived through the shock of her birth, of being born into a world that was cold on the outside as well (she was born in winter in a room that wasn't heated), as well as the pain of having to leave "paradise." She cried for many hours and through tons of tissues, and then she suddenly broke through the illusion—she was connected once again and knew that she had always been connected. She recognized that her feeling of being separated and alone was an illusion. The feeling and knowledge of being connected fulfilled her since it was so natural and obvious. She became calm, thankful, and full of love. The process of healing began within her.

This experience also emphasizes that the essences can trigger processes. The state of being one, which our girlfriend experienced, lasted for several hours and then faded away again. However, it had healed something within her and created a new type of understanding and knowledge. She now knows what her goal is and what it feels like. She has experienced what "oneness" means and can remember it. Now it is more than just abstract knowledge in her head or empty words without contents.

Our girlfriend worked with the *Mary* Essence for three months, until she had the feeling of having cleansed a layer within herself. During this time, she got back together with her boyfriend. The "newly" created relationship is more harmonious, fulfilled, and happier than what both of them had experienced before.

This experience shows once again that reactions can sometimes turn out to be very hefty. As already has been said, it's important not to take direct action and perhaps cause unnecessary trouble that can't be mended again afterwards.

Yet, not every person who uses the essence experiences the pain of separation. Many people who use it report that they achieved a feeling of connectedness and motherly love. They feel themselves to be supported, sustained, and nurtured. And some achieve a deep level of meditation.

Mary also embodies the mother principle, which means giving from the state of abundance and love. This is the motherly, earthly principle. This is also a theme that is frequently misunderstood. People believe that "giving" means saying "yes" to everything and always giving what is demanded and more. They overexert themselves and feel exhausted since they give from their own energy and not from the source. When they stop giving, they become unhappy and weak since giving keeps their energy flowing. With the *Mary* Essence, they learn to connect themselves with the bubbling source and to give from this source. And they learn that giving sometimes also means saying "no" and refusing to give someone else what they want.

People who can naturally live the mother principle, which applies to both men and women, draw from the abundance of the whole and can give selflessly. What we give from a place of love and from the heart enriches ourselves. Then we no longer demand any kind of service in return, no longer need any recognition or attention for it. We can be with others on the basis of the inner source and give them a sense of security, friendliness, and confidence when they need it. We can let them go when they want to go. We are also happy when the others are happy.

The Christian commandment of "love your neighbor as yourself" fits in here since when we have experienced being connected we know that the "neighbor" isn't a separate individual. Instead, everything is interwoven with the same divine quality and everything is influenced by everything else. And then it's also plausible that we must also love ourselves since otherwise this part of the divine fabric would remain unloved. The sense of "being unloved" would flow into the fabric from ourselves.

The Meditation

Vipassana

First step—sitting still

Sit down in the most comfortable position with your back and head upright and your eyes closed. Pay attention to your breathing during the meditation. Observe it without changing it.

In this meditation, it can easily happen that your thoughts wander and that feelings, opinions, bodily sensations, and impressions from the outside world distract you from your breathing. When you become aware that your attention is no longer on your breathing, perceive where you are and return to your breathing. It is the act of observation that counts and not what you observe.

Second step—Vipassana-walking

Walk slowly and normally, directing your attention to how you touch the ground with your feet. Your eyes should be directed to the ground one to two meters ahead of you. While walking, the attention should be focused on each individual foot as it touches the ground. If your attention wanders, look again to see where your thoughts are and return back to your feet with your attention.

The Message

I greet you, and I, who is also called the Mother, am the mother of the earth, the cosmos, the divine, and all being. I connect all things with each other and interweave everything with the divine. My energy makes you aware that everything is interwoven with everything else and that you are a part of the divine, just like every other being and every other existence on this earth. Even the stones and things that you have produced and built— the houses, the cars, the bottles—everything, everything is part of the whole. The vibration of the divine is contained in everything. Although this may be in various forms, the core is still the same.

So I accompany you on this path and open your eyes so that you perceive that you are one with everything and that everything is one with you. Know that you will return back home as a result, that you will acquire consciousness about this, that you participate in the whole and are a part of it, that you will become whole as a result because you can return to your true origin so that you can come into contact with it.

And I support you in translating all of the experiences that you have gained into everyday life, into being. I open up the understanding within you so that all of you can understand this. I am the divine vessel so that the divine flows into me, flows through me, and can distribute itself. This is why you receive access to every direction through me, both to the divine and to the earthly, both to the energies of the cosmic level and to the part on the earth. And you also connect the cosmic, immortal part within yourselves with the earthly aspect. So open yourselves up for the sign of unity. Know how you are connected with each other and recognize where you stand. Open yourselves up for experiencing the divine.

Appendix

Questions and Answers from the Practice

Do the LightBeings Master Essences have an effect on physical complaints?

Physical complaints are an expression of disorders in the harmony of the overall human being, ultimately leading to illness.

The Master Essences harmonize and energize the entire human energy field. When disorders and imbalances are remedied, the body can become healthy once again.

The subtle energies of the LightBeings Master Essences therefore support the body's self-healing powers.

Do I have to believe in the effect for it to be successful?

No. The subtle vibration works even if you don't believe in it and don't feel anything. The precondition is that you are willing to allow an effect.

Even if I don't feel anything, do the Master Essences still have an effect?

Yes. Not all people perceive the subtle energies and vibrations. Even if you don't notice anything, you should continue to use the essence. In order to make a statement about the effect, we recommend that you determine the actual situation before you start to use it. After a period of time, look back at the changes that have taken place inside of you and in your external world such as differences in reactions, how you feel, what you think, whether you come in contact with other types of people, what has happened, etc.

What should I take—the oil, the tincture, or the Master-Energy Ball?

Select whatever appeals to you most. Further criteria for the decision are:

If you want to work more in the emotional or physical area, we recommend the oil. For work in the more subtle areas and on thought patterns, the tincture is recommended.

One further criterion for the decision is the method of application: the oil is applied to the body, which isn't always practical (for example, at work, possible oil spots on clothing). The tincture can be used anywhere at any time during the course of the day and whenever you feel like you need this support.

The Master-Energy Ball should be selected according to the theme that you see as your central theme in life and want to work on intensively. It has its effect through the spiritual aura bodies.

How many different Master Essences can you take at the same time?

More than 3 different Master Essences shouldn't be taken at the same time. It's best to use a combination of tincture and oil.

Can the essences be diluted?

No. The essences are ready for use as they are. A dilution would considerably diminish the effect.

What should I choose if I can't decide on one essence?

This problem occurs frequently when the selection is made using the intellect. We therefore recommend that you let the unconscious mind make the decision through the Master-Essence Card Set or other test procedures (see Chapter 5, *The Selection*, for example).

Is it possible to choose a "wrong" essence?

No, it's not possible to select the "wrong" essence. All of the essence's themes are learning themes for every human being. However, we have already "learned" and integrated these themes to varying degrees. It can be compared with already mastering integral and differential calculus at school but having problems with reading. One essence would further intensify the abilities in integral calculus (progress is naturally not as visible here) and the other helps a person learn to read. The success is much more visible here since this is where the bottleneck is (see Chapter 5 *The Effects*).

How long should I use an essence?

There is no generally valid answer. The length is dependent upon how intense the block or imbalance is, what position the theme has in one's own life plan, the point in time that the essence is used, and how to what extent the person has already integrated the theme into his life.

You will probably use an essence that you have already had at a later time again.

An indication that a theme has been ended for the present time may be that you forget to use the substances and don't feel any desire to use them after a period of intensive application.

Is there always an "initial worsening"?

No, the reaction to the essence depends upon your inner attitude towards the growth process: whether you choose the "steep path" or the "footpath to the peak," how precisely you look at things, your inner resistance, and how you support the process of transformation. It may be that you very quickly achieve the desired positive state when you use the essences.

What should I do if the reaction becomes too hefty for me?

The process of becoming conscious can be supported by the techniques listed in this book (Chapter 5) like "writing lists," candle meditation, or visualization exercises. However, other types of meditation or forms of consciousness work also support the process of more quickly letting go of the inner blocks and coming into a state of balance.

Yet, some people may still feel that it's all too much for them. Then it is advisable to get help from an experienced therapist in whom they trust.

Should I take a break when I have intensively worked through several themes?

It's recommended that you now and then take a break with No. 14—*Victory* in between times. The Victory Essence harmonizes and integrates the learning steps that you have taken into the overall system. It helps you see more clearly where you stand, harmonizing and energizing all of the chakras and energy bodies.

Can my sense of perception change as a result of the Master Essences?

The essences contribute to the expansion of consciousness and you can perceive things that you previously hadn't noticed. Examples of this are that you more quickly recognize behavior patterns in yourself and others, can more clearly see the causes for your own condition, and are able to more "realistically" evaluate other people and situations.

The perception of subtle energies may also develop (opening of the third eye) so that you more easily notice the moods in a room, the feelings and states of other people, the energies at hand in the surrounding world or those you encounter while taking a walk. This isn't always pleasant. Yet, it's also a part of the path to see and accept the world as it is.

What should I do when a bottle has been used up?

Look back to see how you now feel about this theme, what has happened in the meantime, and what further themes have come up as a result. Then you can select the subsequent essences according to the process described in "The Selection."

Can I give an energy ball or bottle that has already been used to someone else?

Yes. All Master Essences and Master-Energy Balls have been energetically sealed, which means that they don't take on any vibrations from the outside. For this reason, bottles that have already been opened can be passed on to other people.

What should I select when I want to give someone else an essence?

Themes that come up for almost every human being time and again are:
No. 2—*Lao Tse*—Inner peace, acceptance. Sometimes it is better to first create the necessary distance to everyday life. In this case, start with No. 1 and then change later to No. 2.
No. 11—*Kuthumi*—Connection to the earth, grounding. Also helps overly rational or unrealistic people.
No. 12—*Lady Nada*—Self-love, feeling accepted, enjoying life.
No. 14—*Victory*—Growth.
    Particularly suitable as a set of three are: No. 8—*Angelica*, No. 9—*Orion*, No. 10—*Kamakura*. This applies especially at the beginning of new projects or phases of life.

Can a person become dependent on the Master Essences?

No. The Master Essences are a support for your own process of becoming conscious and reactivate your own potential. You can compare them with the supporting wheels for a bicycle that helped us learn to ride it. After we learned to keep our balance, we no longer needed the supporting wheels.
    The essences lead to a person's own strength and clarity. As a result, this individual assumes responsibility for himself and consciously takes his life into his own hands. The more he progresses in this process, the more he "becomes himself", the more independent he will be of any type of "outside" help. He masters his own life.

Won't life be boring when I'm completely developed and there's nothing more to do?

From my own experience I can say that my life has become increasingly easier to live the more I develop myself. Today I can accept difficulties much more easily, and with interest and joy, than before. My problems often used to be a catastrophe for me.

My life has become more diversified, colorful, and fulfilled. I live more intensively and can consciously and thankfully enjoy the beauty of life and the joys of the body.

Does a person always have to use the essences when he wants to grow and once he has started using them?

No, the Master Essences are a support on the path to your own mastery. They are *one* form of support. There are many other techniques that are also effective, and each individual can find the methods that best support him. And we naturally also grow without "supporting wheels." However, this "tool" makes the path easier.

If I'm no longer so emotionally entangled because of the essences, won't I be completely indifferent towards everything—won't I be too disassociated and serene?

No, to the contrary—our experiences and the intensity of our life increases. We may also experience feelings more intensely but are no longer at the mercy of mood fluctuations. We become free of the behavior patterns in which we were previously caught and now are free to choose how we will react.

What happens if I just try out the Master Essences?

That depends on your inner willingness to grow. If there is no willingness, nothing will happen. However, if the step in the direction of becoming more conscious is at hand, a process will be set into motion through their use.

The LightBeings Master Essences use the same name in part as Aura-Soma. Are they an imitation of Aura-Soma?

No. The "ascended masters" have come back to the earth in a new form in the LightBeings Master Essences. They work solely through the energy of the masters, which has been bound directly to oil or water. Earthly substances like oil, water, and alcohol only have a carrier function.

The Aura-Soma products have an effect through color, plant energy, and gemstone energy (from Irene Dalichow and Mike Booth

Aura-Soma—*Healing Through Colors, Plant and Gemstone Energies*).

That the names of the LightBeings Master Essences are identical in part with the names of the masters in Aura-Soma is because these are the names of the Ascended Masters. They can also be found in the Theosophical Society, channeled through Helena Blavatsky or in the White Brotherhood. Many mediums are also in contact with them.

The effect of the LightBeings Master Essences and the Aura-Soma Quintessences and Balance Bottles varies even for the same name of a master. This is because the masters have manifest themselves in a new form on the earth.

Perhaps the following image can illustrate the difference:

If we imagine the overall *Christ* consciousness as all the different types of apples, the Aura-Soma Essence would be comparable with the type Red Delicious and the LightBeings *Christ* Essence with Cox Orange. Both types of apples can give us an impression of what apples are, how they taste, and how they are different from pears.

Isn't the effect of the essences and the energy of the masters just imagined? Do these "masters" and other subtle beings exist at all?

These questions and doubts have also come up for us and probably every person time and again, although we have had a great deal of much confirming experience in our process.

Through the way we are raised and life in the Western world, many types of experiences that we have appear to be "unbelievable." Even as children, we learn from adults that our perception of subtle energies and beings is "wrong," that we just imagine it. "Children have a lively imagination," is how they respond.

What is real? We can't answer this question—every person must find the answer for himself. My view of it is: trust in your own experiences and remain critical.

Brief Description
of the Master Energies

No. 1—*Maha Chohan*
Inner Wisdom

The energy of *Maha Chohan* makes it possible for us to take a step back and observe what is happening from the distance, placing experiences, knowledge, and ways of behaving into a new perspective. The distance makes room for inner wisdom.

The energy of *Maha Chohan* is also recommended for people who work with others and give support to others (therapists, counselors, managers).

No. 2—*Lao Tse*
Acceptance and Inner Peace

The energy of *Lao Tse* supports us in accepting ourselves, what happens, and others without condemnation or judgment. "It is like it is." As a result, we can be in the present with attentiveness and composure, recognizing what is valuable in every existence.

This essence makes it possible to experience a deep inner peace, the inner silence.

No. 3—*El Morya*
Trust

The energy of *El Morya* re-establishes the original connection with basic trust: trust in ourselves, trust in our own strength and power, trust in our own divinity and the wisdom of the universe. A person who trusts will experience the power within himself to confidently react in every situation, see events realistically, and remain capable of taking action. He acquires the courage to take action and to have relationships with other human beings.

The essence helps us to overcome fears since fear is often the cause of mistrust.

No. 4—*Kwan Yin*

Dedication

The energy of *Kwan Yin* teaches us dedication to life and to ourselves. In a balanced state, it is possible to flow with life without giving up our own power and strength, still remaining open for experiences and for life. The essence connects us with our own feelings and helps us let bottled-up emotions flow again.

It makes it possible for us to experience the sense of being supported and opens us up for empathy and tolerance towards other beings.

No. 5—*Christ*

Truth and Unconditional Love

Christ teaches "all-encompassing unconditional love." We perceive that this is something other than what is commonly understood to be love.

The *Christ* energy leads to our own truth and supports us in living it, taking clear and strong action from the heart, and occupying our own space. In addition, it is important to ask time and again: "What is my truth and does it correspond with what I do?"

The *Christ* energy supports emotional healing, healing the wounds of the heart, and brings us into contact with the theme of "authority" and the love of fellow beings.

No. 6—*Djwal Khul*

Accepting Your Own Strength

The energy of *Djwal Khul* brings us into contact with our own strength, power, and might. It helps us recognize that we ourselves are the master of our life and create every situation in life ourselves. When a person has recognized this, the possibility opens up for taking full responsibility for his life, using his own strength, and shaping his life as he wants it to be. He accepts his own creative power. Instead of being a victim, he becomes the master of his own fate.

No. 7—*Sanat Kumara*

Connecting Heaven and Earth

The energy of *Sanat Kumara* opens the connection between the "cosmic" and the earthly energy. It strengthens the connection to the physical body, to the three lower energy bodies, and to the earth. By perceiving the divine in the earthly, we are freed of the "burden of earthly existence" and find joy in earthly life. Healing occurs since we accept life on the earth and like to live on the earth.

In people whose vision is restricted to the earth, *Sanat Kumara* also opens up the contact with the "cosmic" energy.

No. 8—*Angelica*

Transforming the Past

Angelica supports us in accepting our own past without judgment. As a result, transformation can occur. Experiences can be integrated into life, and learning steps that haven't yet been completed, that are emotionally difficult, can be ended and therefore become valuable learning experiences.

The treasures that we have collected and buried in the past can then be brought back to the light of day, cleansed, and used in a beneficial way.

No. 9—*Orion*

Visions

Orion helps us recognize our own path in life and receive visions for a path in harmony with the lifeplan.

We see the momentary situations, where we currently stand, what we want to achieve, what experiences and abilities are available to us, what inner blocks hinder our success, what material obstacles are in the way, and what should be done. Order can be brought into the pending steps and then priorities can be set.

The *Orion* energy supports the success of new steps and projects that cover a longer period of time, as well making the daily decisions easier to reach.

No. 10—*Kamakura*

Taking Action

Kamakura helps us to take the steps that we have planned. The energy starts to flow again, blocks are dissolved, and planned steps and concepts are translated into action. We find pleasure in taking action and in being in movement. Even projects that have been put off for a long time can be easily approached and brought to completion.

As a result of the *Kamakura* energy, blocks that have previously stopped us from taking planned steps and taking our life into our hands become conscious.

No. 11—*Kuthumi*

Connecting with the Earth

The energy of *Kuthumi* connects us with the energy of the earth, grounds us, and supports us in coming back into harmony with the earth. It deepens the understanding for correlations and interactions between our body, the aura layers, and the surrounding world, as well as our insight into the processes of nature.

Kuthumi teaches patience and a realistic perception. It becomes more easily possible to see what things are good for us and support us and what should be avoided.

The *Kuthumi* energy also opens up access to wisdom and to the wisdom of the earth.

No. 12—*Lady Nada*

Being Accepted and Enjoying Life

The energy of *Lady Nada* shows the path to unconditional acceptance of ourselves, our body, our existence, our shadow sides, and our strengths. As a result, it supports us in perceiving what joy we can experience within and with the body and what we need to feel good.

This energy makes it possible for us to enjoy life.

It intensifies the sensory perceptions, opens us for the beauty of nature and the world, for music, for fragrances, for pleasant emotional states...

Lady Nada also supports the healing of wounds in sexuality and helps us experience the joy of sexuality.

No. 13—*Seraphis Bey*

The Earthly Power

The energy of *Seraphis Bey* supports us in experiencing, accepting, using, and living our own earthly power. In the process, it supports us in going deep into the energy of the 1st chakra, recognizing, accepting, and integrating its animalistic powers. *Seraphis Bey* brings consciousness into matter.

At the same time, the essence has a cleansing effect and brings light and healing into the shadow aspects of earthly power.

No. 14—*Victory*

Growth

The *Victory* energy supports us on the entire path of development by letting us clearly perceive the momentary situation. It intensifies the flow of energy, harmonizing the energy bodies and all of the chakras with each other. It connects the "feet and the head" and lets us recognize the places where we are blocked, which pattern we can best work on at the moment, and which learning steps are pending. It lets us become aware of problem points.

It is particularly helpful after learning steps have been completed.

No. 15—*Saint Germain*

Freedom

The energy of *Saint Germain* transforms mental and emotional entanglements and helps us perceive and resolve patterns of behavior and negative beliefs. As a result, a new perspective and deeper understanding are possible. We can also get involved in the game of life and enjoy it without getting caught up in it.

This essences leads to inner freedom.

No. 16—*Hilarion*

The Universal Truth

Hilarion helps us to go our own way and see our task and our place in the universe, as well as the universal truth. He makes it possible for us to experience that the individual is reflected in the whole, the microcosm is reflected in the macrocosm, and that our own truth is part of the universal truth.

No. 17—*Pallas Athene*
Joy and Abundance

The energy of *Pallas Athene* supports us in perceiving the inner world, the inner images and feelings, intuition, and our own creative potential—and then translate all of this into action. It connects creativity with taking action and with structure, leading to an expression of inner abundance and beauty. It becomes possible for us to spontaneously express our feelings and emotions. It opens the flow of joy in life and playfulness, letting life become a spirited, joyful dance.

No. 18—*Lady Portia*
Being Balanced

The *Lady Portia* energy helps us reach our own inner balance between the poles, our own inner center. This results in the creation of an inner harmony, peace, and a state of balance so that we succeed in being or becoming composed and clear even in difficult circumstances. We use events that shake us up to achieve a new equilibrium.

This essence also supports the harmony between the immortal and the earthly aspects of our being.

No. 19—*Helion*
Being Like the Sun

Our own divine beings is like the warming, luminous rays of the sun. The essence of *Helion* supports us in discovering, experiencing, and living our inner light and shining to the outside world through our own way of "being as we are." It leads to self-love and lets our own charisma come alive.

No. 20—*Aeolus*
Recognizing the Creator within Ourselves

The energy of Aeolus connects us with our consciousness and our creative powers of the divine. We perceive the correlations between our inner state and the outer world, the connection between our thinking, feeling, wishes and fears and the things that happen. As a result, it becomes clear to us that we ourselves are the creator of our life and we discern the laws of the creative process.

No. 21—*Mary*

Perceiving the Unity

The energy of *Mary* helps us dissolve the illusion of separation by opening us up to the experience of being connected with everything. We realize that we have always been accepted and have been in the love and will remain in it. She envelops us in all-encompassing love, protection, and security. We can become whole within her and once again open ourselves up for our love, for our own light.

We can also recognize that all people search for the same thing. As a result, we can encounter people in a different way. We can more easily give and permit closeness, friendship, and love.

Pendulum Table

From: *"Pendel-Welten" (Pendulum Worlds)* by Markus Schirner,
Schirner Verlag, Darmstadt, Germany.

The Authors

© by Foto-Atelier Launer

Dr. Petra Schneider, born in 1960, studied and received her doctor's degree in the subject of agronomy at the University of Bonn. In 1990, she completed additional training for the teaching profession, administrative work, and consultation and accepted a position as an official at the Agricultural Chamber. There she dealt with questions related to environmental protection in agriculture and the topics of brown coal and village development.

During this time she became intensely interested in the meaning of her life. As a result, she realized that her professional activities didn't provide fulfillment for her life. She quit the secure, life-long position and began a deep involvement with subtle energies, meditation, and the possibilities of holistic development of the self. Among other things, one aspect of this was training to become a Reiki teacher, NLP practitioner, and meditation teacher.

She now works as a holistic personal counselor and gives seminars.

Since 1994 she has been intensely involved with the energies of the Ascended Masters, resulting in the creation of the Light-Beings Master Essences.

Gerhard K. Pieroth, born in 1956, is a certified industrial engineer and worked as an employee of the computer manufacturer IBM in the production, marketing, and sales departments. As a secondary occupation, he was a lecturer at several institutes of higher learning.

In 1988, the failure of his marriage and collapse of his world view lead him on the search for meaning in his life and brought his first experiences with meditation. He opened up increasingly to the abilities he hadn't lived out before that point and quit his job in 1992. Then he trained to be a Reiki teacher and NLP practitioner, among other things. Parallel to this, he trained in the field of adult education and currently works as a holistic success and management consultant, as well as a coach and trainer at companies and for individuals.

Together with Petra, he produces the LightBeings Master Essences and holds seminars.

Expression of Thanks

During the entire phase in which the Master Essences and this book were created, we received help from not only "non-physical" beings but also from many "physical beings."

In the first place, we would like to thank Friederike Quest and Hubert Peters from the bottom of our hearts. Both have encouraged and vigorously supported us from the very first charging process up to the present. And although they had very little time themselves, they did the proofreading and gave us valuable suggestions.

We would also like to thank Isis Herzog, who enriched this book through her journalistic abilities, her experience, and her many ideas.

We would also like to thank Markus Schirner for the valuable, practical information he gave us and for contributing to the process of turning the idea into reality.

Last but not least, we also thank our friend Aseema Wunderle for her support. I learned channeling through her.

There were naturally many other people as well who supported us through their feedback on the effects and their suggestions. We thank them as well.

Sources of Supply:

The following companies have an extensive selection of useful products and a long track-record of fulfillment. They have natural body care, aromatherapy, flower essences, crystals and tumbled stones, homeopathy, herbal products, vitamins and supplements, videos, books, audio tapes, candles, incense and bulk herbs, teas, massage tools and products and numerous alternative health items across a wide range of categories.

WHOLESALE:

Wholesale suppliers sell to stores and practitioners, not to individual consumers buying for their own personal use. Individual consumers should contact the RETAIL supplier listed below. Wholesale accounts should contact with business name, resale number or practitioner license in order to obtain a wholesale catalog and set up an account.

Lotus Light Enterprises, Inc.

P O Box 1008 LB
Silver Lake, WI 53170 USA
414 889 8501 (phone)
414 889 8591 (fax)
800 548 3824 (toll free order line)

RETAIL:

Retail suppliers provide products by mail order direct to consumers for their personal use. Stores or practitioners should contact the wholesale supplier listed above.

Internatural

33719 116th Street LB
Twin Lakes, WI 53181 USA
800 643 4221 (toll free order line)
414 889 8581 office phone
WEB SITE: www.internatural.com

Web site includes an extensive annotated catalog of more than 7000 products that can be ordered "on line" for your convenience 24 hours a day, 7 days a week.